Historic Landscapes of the Great Orme

Historic Landscapes of the Great Orme

Early Agriculture and Copper-mining

by Mary Aris

editor Capell Aris

GWASG Carreg Gwalch

Cyhoeddwyr ac Argraffwyr

Aerial photography by Mary and Capell Aris
Design and computerized production
by Capell Aris

Cover photo: early landscape at Hwylfa'r Ceirw, Great Orme, Llandudno.

ISBN 0-86381-357-7

First published in 1996 by Gwasg Carreg Gwalch,
Iard yr Orsaf, Llanrwst, Wales, 01492 642031

Printed and published in Wales

Contents

Aerial photography and historic landscape on the Great Orme 7

Geology 13

The agrarian background in Creuddyn 19

The quest for copper 29

Aspects of mining 35

Two eras of mining at Pyllau 51

Early agriculture and industry at Hwylfa'r Ceirw 59

Open field farming, settlement and mining near St Tudno's Church .. 67

Agriculture, settlement and mining near Mynydd Isaf 77

Mining landscapes at Bryniau Poethion 83

Agricultural change on the Great Orme 89

The landscape of mining 97

Postscript 101

Acknowledgements 105

Notes and references 107

Legend to diagrams 112

Index.. 113

The Great Orme's Head, Llandudno. The English version of the name is derived from a Viking place-name. The headland acted as a important landmark to Vikings navigating the Irish Sea basin. The Welsh name is Pen y Gogarth.

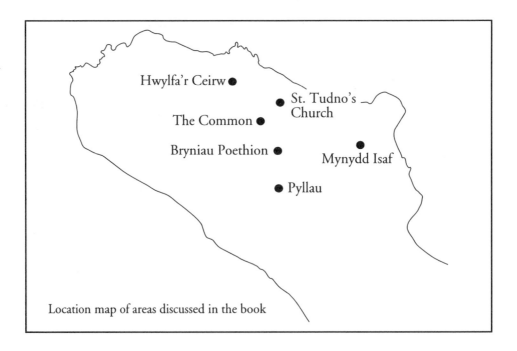

Hwylfa'r Ceirw ●

● St. Tudno's Church

The Common ●

Bryniau Poethion ●

● Mynydd Isaf

● Pyllau

Location map of areas discussed in the book

1

Aerial Photography and Historic Landscape on the Great Orme

THE PEOPLES of the past have not disappeared without trace—they have left their imprint behind them. To find out more about their lives and activities, we have to examine evidence from the past. Several kinds of evidence can offer information. Written documents are useful, but these are most plentiful only for the last few centuries. As one looks further back in time, archive sources become scanty and eventually non existent. Buried artefacts, from archaeological sites and from underground exploration (for mining history), provide another source. But there is further evidence etched into the landscape itself. People change their environment. Human activity in agriculture or industry creates subtle landscape changes. The pioneering local historian W. E. Hoskins used to insist that the landscape was a sort of document, if only we could learn its language or read its message:

> *'Everything in our present landscape tells us something about the past if only we can learn how to interpret it.'*

Many techniques have been employed by landscape historians. This book is going to explore one approach. It will show how aerial photography can assist in the process of interpreting the landscape. By examining some selected aerial photographs, analysing their evidence, and where possible comparing their record against the evidence from other approaches, the book will offer a key to help unlock the messages hidden in our landscapes.

The focus of this book is historic landscape on the Great Orme. Only from the air is it possible to appreciate the remarkable amount of ancient landscape that survives at Llandudno. Aerial photography can highlight a remarkable degree of detail. It is a valuable method of investigation for the historian of landscape change. From the air it is sometimes possible to perceive patterns and appreciate features that may be unclear on the ground. A light aircraft can cover the ground quickly and effectively, allowing the comparison of different features. The oblique photography that can be obtained is particularly useful for archaeology.

The landscape has sometimes been described as a palimpsest. Its surface has been erased and overwritten many times over. In places, however, the underlying evidence of former activity has not been completely erased. But how and why have traces of earlier landscape survived here? The Great Orme at Llandudno is fortunate because it is a 'marginal' area in terms of soils and agriculture. Rising steeply to 679 feet, it is exposed to the full blast of the prevailing south westerly winds, and has not seen the intensive, ongoing agricultural use of more sheltered lowland areas. This has been a vital factor in ensuring the survival of its remarkable expanses of ancient landscape.

The photograph opposite shows a system of fields or strips, separated by low walls or banks. From the ridged nature of the ground it is clear that this area, which has long been open common, was at one time ploughed. This in itself raises interesting questions about changes in farming practice through the centuries. What date is it? When was this system of fields laid out? What sort of people farmed here? How were they organized? Did they live in the structures whose foundations we can see outlined so clearly at the head of the strips? And why were the lands eventually abandoned? We will try to answer some of these questions later in the book, but before we can reach a real understanding of landscape changes at Llandudno, we need to explore and analyse some of the surviving areas of historic landscape. We need to look at the ways in which it has been altered. We may need to compare and contrast different types of landscape. We will also try to interpret what we find in the light of other available evidence.

Aerial photographs force us to think about the processes of landscape change. They offer visible evidence that landscapes and land use in the past must have been very different from those visible today.
Landscape provides a most remarkable historical record. On its surface it

Opposite: medieval field system on the common

preserves remarkably detailed evidence of past human activity. Whenever people carry out activities like ploughing or mining or quarrying, the land may never be quite the same again. Aerial photography allows us to seek out and record some of these traces of former activity. Let us see in this book what it can tell us about agriculture and industry at Llandudno. The book will focus on five key areas of historic landscape. These have been chosen for their remarkable degree of detail, and because they give unique insights into agricultural or mining activity on the Great Orme. All the chosen locations are also complex landscapes which offer evidence of activity for more than one period. Because of that they have a special value in elucidating some of the processes of landscape change that have taken place at Llandudno. This book is going to examine some odd corners of the Great Orme, and some out of the way areas, because it is often in apparently insignificant places that most clues remain.

There are subtle clues hidden in the landscape which can show what former peoples did and how they used the natural resources they found around them. People remake their environment. Different generations use resources in a different way. But they do not always obliterate all traces of what has gone before. Underneath the present day landscape, under the tight knit turf of this limestone plateau there are the shadows of earlier landscapes. At times it is almost as if we could see layers, or eras, of human activity etched there. Through the aerial photographs in this book we are going to begin the task of analysing and disentangling some of these layers. Of course aerial photography has limitations and cannot provide all the answers. It offers the historian one approach. There is also a need to look at what other methods of investigation can contribute—ground survey, excavation, use of documents, maps and photographs in the archives, and of course, in this case underground exploration. Sometimes there will be agreement between these approaches. Different methods often complement each other. At other times, however, it may well be that the landscape evidence provides the only surviving record. An aerial photograph offers a unique viewpoint. It provides a fresh starting point. It is probably the single most important record for the landscape historian.

Llandudno's remarkable historic landscapes deserve to be far more widely known. Much of the material published here has not to my knowledge been made available before. I hope it will increase understanding of this fascinating, complex area and the changes that have affected its landscape over time.

Geology provided the stage, but agriculture and industry have been the twin forces that have shaped the landscape of the Great Orme.

The Great Orme

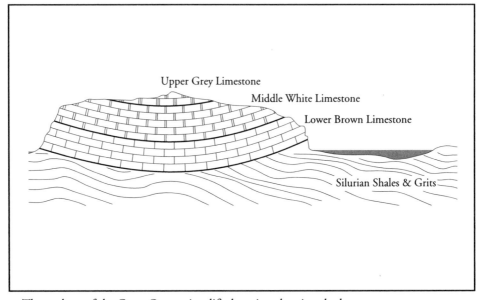

The geology of the Great Orme: simplified section showing the layers

2

Geology

GEOLOGY has had a vital influence on both agricultural and mining activity. The Great Orme's Head is an isolated limestone promontory thrusting out into the Irish Sea. In area it is approximately two miles long and a mile wide. Its limestone strata were formed on the floor of a warm, shallow, tropical sea (rather like the Gulf of Florida today). The seabed was vast and the same limestone occurs in the Clwydian Hills and as far east as Shropshire. The sedimentary layers are the compressed remains of the shells and skeletons of countless small marine creatures accumulating over a vast span of geological time. Many of the quarry faces contain fossil evidence. There are three distinct layers, the Upper Grey, the Middle White and the Lower Brown. The rocks that now form the Great Orme were later uplifted to become dry land. During this process, the layered limestone beds, contorted by immense pressures in the earth's crust, have been squeezed and folded into a gentle syncline. Faulting has also occurred. Rock has fractured along the lines of pressure and along the bedding joints [1].

Other powerful geological forces were at work to change these rocks. The forces caused by the earth's plate tectonics generated huge pressures and temperatures high enough to liquefy rock. The sedimentary rocks forming the Great Orme were to be further altered by the upwelling of hot, mineral-rich liquids forced up under tremendous pressures from deep within the earth's crust. In the lower section of the second layer some of the limestone has been chemically changed to magnesium limestone or dolomite. It is in this layer of crystalline rock that the greatest mineralization has occurred.

The layered nature of the strata can be seen clearly in the cliff near Happy Valley. On close examination some surface evidence of small scale mining activity is also visible.

This mineral grant is more than a square mile, and has running through it from north to south two mineral channels of ground from 30 to 40 fathoms wide containing a great number of parallel veins and strings nearly vertical, also cross and oblique veins underlaying at different angles, and a great number of beds horizontal from east to west and dipping northward . . . On the junction of these veins with the vertical veins very rich bunches of ore have been found and worked.

A Victorian mine-surveyor's description of the underground seams at Llandudno, 1846 [2]

Fault lines and bedding joints influenced the process of mineralization, as the hot, mineral rich liquids surged up and sought out the weaknesses and joints in the rock. In the major fault lines in particular and at their intersections minerals were deposited as lodes of ore, crystalline rock and aggregate. At the intersection of veins the mineralization is exceptionally rich. One of the most productive sectors through the ages has been below the Pyllau area, where the 'hanging vein' and the Cyllell or 'Knife vein' intersect. Further east in north Wales, silver and lead are mined, but at Llandudno the mineralization was mainly of copper, a highly pure form of copper with a low arsenic content. Only very small quantities of lead and other minerals were sold from the Llandudno mines.

One major series of fault lines runs north to south from Gogarth to near Saint Tudno's Church. This belt has seen the most intensive mining activity, and is of special importance. The earliest known copper-mining site, and one of the most productive, is on a major fault in the Pyllau valley. There are also a number of lesser, east to west faults which have seen smaller scale exploitation.

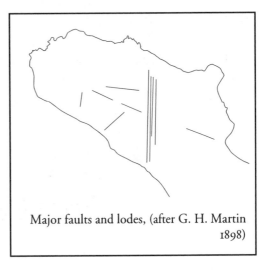

Major faults and lodes, (after G. H. Martin 1898)

Generally dolomite limestone is hard. However, around areas of mineralization, the rock is softer. At depths copper ores occur locked as sulphides. Copper iron pyrites (chalcopyrite) has a brassy golden colour somewhat similar to 'fools gold' in appearance. Sulphide ores require high temperatures and complicated roasting processes to smelt. In the higher layers, the copper ores also exist as carbonates. Malachite ore is blue, green or turquoise in colour, and would have been visible as eye-catching streaks of colour in the rocks. Copper ore also occurs in the Great Orme in a third form: as small blue platelets of azurite flakes in grey rock. Again, these are colourful, highly visible ores, which may well have been exploited by the first miners.

Carbonates of copper can be smelted at a temperature of 985 °C, temperatures which could be attained in primitive furnaces with the aid of some ventilation. Natural raw copper (tenorite) can also occur in limestone, suspended as tiny fragments, and cuprite (copper oxide) is also found.

Water was to play a part in shaping this distinctive limestone plateau although on the surface it is the apparent lack of water that is such a distinctive feature of limestone geology. Because carboniferous limestone is porous, water in limestone country behaves in odd ways. Although there was once surface water, by now streams have vanished below ground leaving only dry valleys and gulleys. Surface drainage water percolates slowly through joints and solution holes. As it sinks, it seeks out points of weakness in the the bedding joints, and faults in the rock layers, enlarging the fissures over time. Drainage water would seek out out those same faults and lines of weakness up which the hot liquids from the earth's crust had once surged.

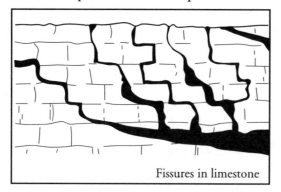

Fissures in limestone

Limestone is often honeycombed with sink holes, and underground caverns. Water occurs in subterranean channels at Llandudno [3]. Rumblings of trickling underground streams produced mysterious noises. These haunted the superstitious Llandudno miners, giving rise to stories of 'Knockers'. Water also drips slowly from the roof of caverns to form stalactites and strange branching formations. Some of these grow at only a few millimetres per century. Massive stalactites were occasionally found by the nineteenth century miners.

'I remember seeing hanging from the roof big stalactites, like branches of trees, which had been formed by water penetrating the roof.'

John Hughes, ex copper-miner, 1917 [4]

On the surface limestone holds other surprises, with unexpected hidden springs and wells, where an impervious layer of rock forces the water to the surface. The vegetation of herbs and grasses and abundant wild flowers is sweet but sparse. Grasses and flowers grow in fissures between the clints in areas of exposed limestone pavement.

Water, ice and weather have affected the Great Orme. Surrounded on three sides by sea, its impressive cliffs are subject to an ongoing process of erosion. Carboniferous limestone is soft, soluble in water, and easily eroded. This results in a highly distinctive geology. Layers of rock are exposed in steep cliffs or tiered scarps. The ground falls steeply in most places on all four sides of the Orme. On the plateau there are areas of exposed limestone pavement, tiered scarps, and steep gulleys. But it is the towering limestone cliffs that are perhaps the most distinctive feature. The cliffs, sheer in many places, isolate the plateau making it a world apart. Access onto the Great Orme has always been tortuous and difficult. Its limestone walls make it into a natural fortress. This has been a factor of tremendous importance in preserving the expanses of ancient landscape there, as if in a time capsule.

Limestone cliffs on the Great Orme

Some of the natural features of the limestone geology may have assisted the earliest searchers after metals. In places erosion and the after effects of glaciation produced natural caves in the cliffs. Limestone caves are known to have provided shelter for hunter/gatherer peoples more than ten thousand years ago. After the glacial period there would have been many more caves and fissures than we see today, as a result of the erosive power of glacial streams and melt-water. Potholes, fissures and natural caves might have provided easy access ways into the bowels of the earth, revealing as colourful streaks in their soft limestone walls the mineral riches of the Orme, which had been deposited there far back in geological time.

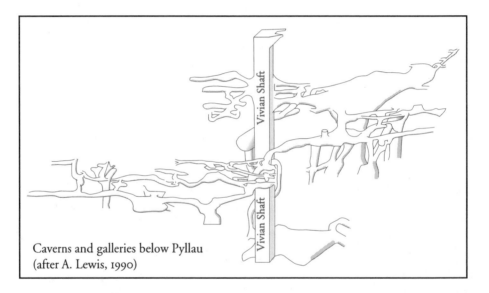

Caverns and galleries below Pyllau
(after A. Lewis, 1990)

Natural geology may even account for some of the extensive caverns found underground, which are currently ascribed entirely to Bronze Age mining activity. Bronze Age copper-mining at Llandudno penetrated to far greater depths than, for instance, those attained by neolithic flint miners at Grimes Graves in Norfolk, mining in chalk, with similar primitive bone, stone and wooden tools. It is possible that some at least of the underground chambers represent natural fissures which could have been worked and enlarged by human agency in the extraction of mineral ores. Some caverns bear a striking resemblance to natural passages or pipes [5], although it is generally claimed that there are no underground cave systems at Llandudno.

3

The Agrarian Background in Creuddyn

ARCHAEOLOGICAL evidence at Llandudno testifies to human occupation over a long timespan. Evidence of early cave dwellers was discovered at Kendrick's cave in 1879. The first peoples were hunters and gatherers, but farming and cultivation probably began around 4500 BC in the Neolithic period. There is a fine neolithic burial chamber, Llety'r Filiast, at Maes y Facrell. Burial monuments such as these may have had an important function in asserting the rights of a particular group of people to farm a particular area of land [1]. There have been Bronze Age finds at Llandudno.

The fine Iron Age hillfort of Pen y Dinas contains numerous hut circles, and there is considerable evidence of Roman activity in the Llandudno area, especially in the third century. Evidence for medieval settlement continues with long huts and a later platform house. By inference, since neolithic times there must have been farming activity on and around the Great Orme.

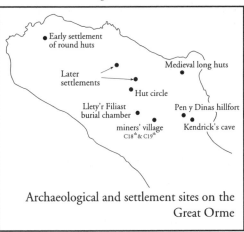

Archaeological and settlement sites on the Great Orme.

Other shadowy evidence lurks in legend and local oral tradition, until firm documentary evidence finally emerges after the conquest of Gwynedd in 1283.

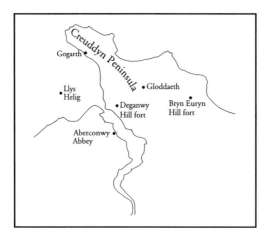

There are legends of the loss of fertile lands nearby to the sea: the Dark Age palace of Llys Helig, and lands around it are said to have suffered inundation by the waves. Tradition also speaks of an early religious foundation at Gogarth, which may have been an abbey or a nunnery, and which is said to have later become attached to the abbey of Aberconwy.

The Great Orme lies in close proximity to hill forts and royal *maerdref* sites at Deganwy and Bryn Euryn, important residences of the rulers of Gwynedd since at least the time of Maelgwn Gwynedd in the sixth century. Gogarth might at one time have had some role as part of the the food producing lands which victualled the royal court in the era of the early Welsh princes. It lies adjacent to the power centre of Pen y Dinas hillfort. Several widely scattered groups of villeins owed labour service at Gogarth [2]. For instance bond tenants at the township of Garthgogo, near Abergele, beside the ancient hill fort of Pen y Corddyn Mawr, had to do three days labour service at Gogarth. Following excavations at Gogarth [3], Douglas Hague the excavator suggested there was a possibility, that one substantial building with impressive architecture (which escaped destruction during the Glyndŵr uprising when other buildings on the site were torched) might represent earlier native workmanship, and could have belonged to the earlier period of the Princes.

During the two hundred year struggle between the Normans and the Welsh, the castle nearby at Deganwy, controlling the coastal access route into the kingdom of Gwynedd was in the front line. The site changed hands many times. Welsh tactics in the face of superior military forces were often to evacuate men and livestock from a threatened area, to the uplands of Snowdonia, then wage guerilla warfare. The local population at Llandudno, near to this hotly contested area, cannot have been unaffected by the tides of warfare or the depredations and reprisals of occupying Norman garrisons.

The manor of Gogarth lying east of the River Conwy was among the lands sequestered by the English Crown after the war of 1277. It was granted by Edward I to Anian, Bishop of Bangor, a cleric who was noted for his preference for an Anglicized lifestyle and practice. This grant to the Church may well have been part of Edward I's carefully structured moves to win the support of the powerful Welsh Church for the new settlement. As Lord of the Manor of Gogarth the Bishop owned a substantial palace just below the Great Orme. He exacted his dues and exercised his authority over his tenants.

Only after the Edwardian conquest does the first detailed documentary evidence survive for the manor of Gogarth and the Great Orme. A collection of surveys made in 1294, 1306, 1348/9 and 1352, known as *The Record of Caernarvon*, [4], is in many respects the Principality's equivalent to the more famous Domesday survey for England. In many respects these surveys raise as many questions as they answer. However, they do offer a 'snapshot' of north Wales just after the Edwardian conquest. They provide an important record of medieval land tenure and custom at one particular point in time. The Bishop's manor of Gogarth included three townships at Llandudno—Gogarth in the south, below the Orme, Cyngreawdr, probably in the northern sector of the Orme near Saint Tudno's Church, and Yr Wyddfid in the east. In addition to giving details of the rents payable each year, the 1306 survey gives valuable information about other feudal dues

and about the nature of tenure. At Gogarth township all but one of the manor's thirteen tenants owed certain dues and services to the Lord, including labour service, suit of court, and the obligation to grind their corn at the Lord's windmill, in addition to their annual cash rents. They held under a bond tenure. One other free tenant at Gogarth held two houses and land under a less burdensome

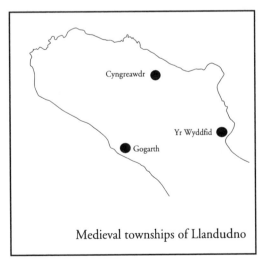

Medieval townships of Llandudno

tenure without the customary obligations, perhaps representing some more recent grant. In the township of Cyngreawdr, there were a number of free tenants who seem to have had exceptional privileges. Two tenants and their sub-tenants held six houses and land. These tenants paid no rents and owed suit of court only. They also had the right to sue in another court elsewhere, if they preferred. These lenient terms of tenure might have represented an inducement to settle there. In the bond township of Yr Wyddfid, the manorial dues were heavier. Tenants of seven houses and lands were noted as being 'in villeinage', owing, rents, labour service and suit of court and mill, and there were two other tenants at will with similar obligations, one of whom was a miller. In one brief but vivid word picture, the survey also mentions a windmill at Gogarth with broken sails. Presumably it stood somewhere on the Great Orme itself to catch the wind.

These townships at Llandudno were characterized by their small size, compared to surrounding townships. They were also comparatively fortunate, for in many respects they were less heavily burdened with customary dues and services, than certain other townships in the survey, (especially bond townships) which had heavy obligations imposed upon them, such as fines on the marriage of a daughter or the succession by heirs on the death of the original holder. In the rest of Creuddyn as in most of the Principality, a mixture of bond and free townships existed by the time of the conquest. The last Welsh princes had begun modernizing their state, introducing new forms of tenure probably at some time in the twelfth or very early thirteenth century. (Only the adjoining commote of Nant Conway had an unusually high proportion of bond tenants [5]).

Minister's accounts of taxes collected by the Sheriff offer some insights into agrarian hardship in Creuddyn in other areas still retained by the Crown, and show how Welsh tenants fared under the new regime. Edward I introduced a wholesale money economy. Food renders and services which had customarily been paid in kind were commuted to a money charge. In practice this meant that tenants had to exchange their produce and sell livestock to obtain cash to pay their dues. However, buying and selling was now forbidden outside of official markets. The new Anglicized boroughs established by Edward I held a monopoly over the markets, and extracted heavy tolls from farmers. Farmers in Creuddyn would have been obliged to buy and sell their produce in the 'official' market in the new Borough of Conwy.

Pestilence in the mid fourteenth century compounded this economic hardship. Many populations were decimated by the Black Death which reached north Wales in the summer of 1349. The after-effects of the plague bore particularly hard on bond townships, where survivors remained collectively liable for the entire dues of the township, an impossible commitment when much land was lying uncultivated from lack of the labour to work it. The Glyndŵr wars of rebellion after 1400 also caused dislocation, devastation and reprisal. The effects of war were felt in the heart of the Creuddyn peninsular. Part of Gogarth Palace was itself burned [6]. War added to existing impoverishment and economic distress. By 1410, all over the county villeins were fleeing from economic oppression. After the Glyndŵr uprising, Creuddyn was treated with extreme harshness. In other areas the burden of taxes was lessened but in Creuddyn the Crown attempted to extort the full burden of payments, though the impoverished commote could raise only one sixth of the cash demanded [7]. By the time of Henry VI, there were no villeins in Creuddyn and Nant Conwy (bond land had escheated through lack of tenants) and an act of 1507 recognized reality by abolishing bond status in the three shires of north Wales.

The Bishops of Bangor in their capacity as Lord of the Manor of Gogarth would have been equally intent on making as much profit out of the manor

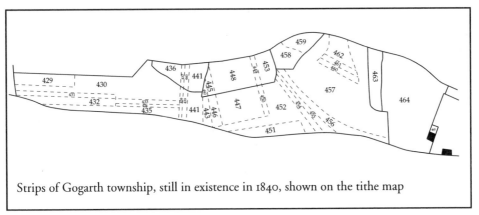

Strips of Gogarth township, still in existence in 1840, shown on the tithe map

as possible, and jealously guarded their property and rights. The Bishop was to have an important interest throughout the centuries in the Great Orme, until the Church finally relinquished ownership of Gogarth in 1891. Manorial courts enforced the Bishop's rights, and extorted payments due to the Lord of the Manor. They dealt with cases of trespass and regulated many of the agricultural operations at Llandudno, especially in an era when open field farming meant that many of the operations of ploughing, sowing and harvesting and pasturing stock had to be synchronized. Following the Civil War of 1642 to 1646, during the Inter-Regnum, Gogarth was sequestered and sold to the Parliamentarian, John Jones of Maes y Garnedd [8], but the property was restored to the Church on the accession of Charles II in 1660. Despite its apparent isolation and tranquil setting, this area was not immune from periods of turbulence and hardship.

Another major player was to be the acquisitive and powerful family at Gloddaeth. They held a family seat and landed estates in Llandudno. Already by the mid fifteenth century Gruffudd ap Rhys of Gloddaeth, (who died in 1480) held some lands of the Bishop in the township of Cyngreawdr on the Great Orme. The heiress to his estates, Margaret, brought together the important estates of Gloddaeth, and Mostyn by her first marriage just before 1465. Margaret herself, a remarkable woman, seems to have started the process of estate building and pursued a policy of purchasing lands which adjoined those already in her possession. She acquired further lands at Cyngreawdr [9]. The Mostyn family, who also had extensive holdings further east in Flintshire, were one of the important gentry families in north Wales. The development of a land market, the later breakdown of the bond townships, and under the Tudors the 'privatisation' of monastery lands, boosted the economic status of the gentry. They flourished in the era of estate building under the Tudors and Stuarts. Their economic stature increased even further in the early industrial period, as they began to develop industries on their estates. Certainly the Mostyns seem to have been acquisitive and hungry for land and estates. In the sixteenth century the Bishop seems to have farmed out the manor and its courts and profits, retaining only the palace under direct episcopal control [10]. The Mostyns frequently leased the manor from him, exercising the function of Lord of the Manor in all but name.

In consolidating their estates landowners eventually began to enclose blocks of strips and bought out other lesser interests in the process of blocking up their holdings. By the seventeenth century, they had begun a process of enclosure of holdings on the Great Orme, which eventually became individual farms. There are several references in seventeenth century estate deeds to 'closes' at Llandudno. Through their acquisitive enclosing activities, the Mostyn Estate even incurred the wrath of the Bishop of Bangor. An episcopal survey of 1680 complained about the enclosing activities of the Mostyn estate altering the face of the Great Orme. The traditional boundaries were *so utterly broke up that it is impossible to find them out* [11]. The new spirit of individualism led to the replacement of areas of open fields by individual farms, owning their land in tight blocks. By the mid eighteenth century enclosure of some of the most agriculturally valuable parts of the Great Orme was considerably advanced. A deed of 1761 mentioned 28 closes at Llandudno [12]. By then the farms of Pyllau, Maes y Facrell, Llwyn Helyg, Ty'n-y-coed and Ty'n yr Hendre and Penmynydd had emerged in the eastern sector. The process did not encompass the whole of the Orme. Most of the land lying to the west was open common. By the early nineteenth century, the Mostyns were active, draining marshy land at the base of the Orme. Enclosure was to be important, not only because it allowed agricultural improvements and individual farming methods, but also because it gave control over valuable mineral deposits.

Gloddaeth

The core of the manorial holding of Gogarth was the fertile, lower lying land below the Orme. Almost certainly it was more extensive than the narrow coastal strip visible today. Land has been lost as a result of the action of the River Conwy inexorably cutting its channel ever further northwards. A sea chart of 1748 by William Morris shows Gogarth Abbey about a mile inland. Loss of land was to continue relentlessly. Even in 1907, local residents could remember that, within living memory, ploughing had extended more than 200 yards from the base of the cliffs.

Creuddyn generally was noted as a great corn growing area. Peter Bailey Williams in 1820 praised its excellent wheat [13]. The lowland strip of Gogarth was particularly renowned for its fertile soils. Thomas Pennant in 1777 described Gogarth as 'a long but narrow tract of great fertility'. The upland hinterland was of lower agricultural potential. By the eighteenth century the Great Orme was largely used for sheep raising. Pennant described it as 'a beautiful sheepwalk of fine turf'. An annual sheep fair was held at Llandudno. Stone sheep pens at Yr Wyddfid were used for this purpose.

The Llandudno Tithe Map and Survey provides another important 'snapshot' of agriculture on and around the great Orme in 1840. Unusually this Tithe Apportionment predates the Enclosure Award for the area. By 1840 the Mostyn estate had gained control of considerable lands around the base of the Orme. On the Orme itself they owned several important farms. Even in 1840, the very last vestiges of a former medieval landscape and strip field system had not been completely obliterated. Some strips are still recognisable, and many were still only delineated by low baulks (shown on the maps by a dotted line), though others had been enclosed and fossilized with stone walls.

An important influence on the landscape in the eighteenth and nineteenth centuries was the growth of a mining settlement in the eastern sector of the Orme. Down the steep valley below Pyllau and around Maes y Facrell emerged a distinctive pattern of miners' cottages, many with large gardens or allotments. These were built along blocks of land of earlier medieval strips. The former pattern of strip fields can still be discerned in the pattern of the streets at Yr Wyddfid, and traces of rig and furrow are still visible. Miners at Llandudno valued their small plots of ground, which supplemented their fluctuating wages, and provided an insurance against hard times. There was a strong smallholding tradition in the mining community. In spite of the growth of industrialization, the men had not lost their ties with the land, and the hours at the mine (a six hour day even in the nineteenth century) gave them time to cultivate their gardens and smallholdings [14]

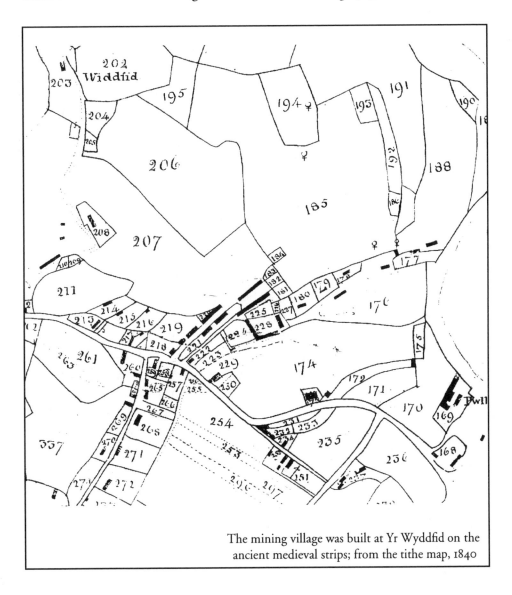

The mining village was built at Yr Wyddfid on the ancient medieval strips; from the tithe map, 1840

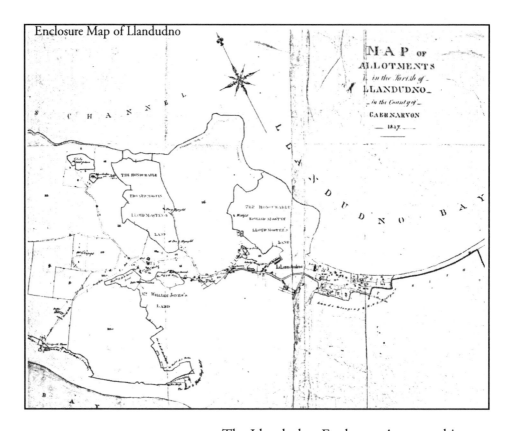

Enclosure Map of Llandudno

The Llandudno Enclosure Act passed in 1843 brought further agricultural changes on the Great Orme after its implementation in 1847, though its impact on the low lying sandy tract between the Great and Little Orme was to be even greater. There the Mostyn Estate gained control of virtually all of the area now occupied by the present town of Llandudno and systematically began to develop the area as a holiday resort and watering place. On the Great Orme an extensive area near the summit was parcelled out into large fields and enclosed, and formed the farm of Parc.

4

The Quest for Copper

Early mining

RECENT discoveries have provided important evidence for Bronze Age copper-mining at Llandudno, both on the surface and underground. There have been finds of bone and stone tools (many of them carrying wear marks on one edge), two small fragments of copper, together with charcoal which has yielded radio carbon dates in the range 1800–500 BC. Many of the finds have been in sealed layers. On the surface these were preserved under later spoil heaps. Underground they were covered in a layer of calcite that differentiated them from more recent material [1].

Some doubt has been cast on the claims for Bronze Age mining, because it is known that, on limestone, charcoal and settlement refuse can sometimes work their way underground through solution holes in the limestone which can develop below early settlement sites [2]. However, enough evidence from many different locations does now seem to substantiate Bronze Age mining at Llandudno. Whether this early mining was on the massive scale postulated by some authorities remains to be proved. Some of the apparently large underground workings may be natural caverns, perhaps enlarged by early miners. Initially the mining was interpreted as belonging to one intensive period of activity with an operation on a massive scale[3]. As further evidence emerged certain archaeologists modified their views, because of the spread of radio-carbon dates, and some now view the mining as a lower key activity, perhaps even seasonal working, spread over a wider period of time [4].

Nineteenth century miners certainly believed in the existence of ancient mines, though they ascribed these to 'the Romans' rather than to any earlier period. On occasions later miners broke into large caverns in the course of their operations.

Interesting Discovery of a Cavern in Wales

On Wednesday the miners at Llandudno broke in the course of their labours into what appears to be an extensive cavern, the roof of which being one mass of stalactite reflected back their lights with dazzling splendour.

On examination the cavern turned out to be an old work, probably Roman, the benches, stone hammers etc. used by that ancient people having been found entire, together with many bones of mutton, which had been consumed by those primitive miners. The bones are to all appearances fresh, though impregnated with copper, as they were when denuded of their fleshy covering, after remaining nearly 2,000 years in the bowels of the earth. The cavern is about 40 yards long and must be a subject of great interest to those fond of investigating the remains of bygone ages.

Liverpool Mercury, 1849

Where fragments of copper tools were found in 1831 and 1849 we can say with some confidence in at least two cases that they were genuine mine workings.

There is only slight evidence for copper-mining at Llandudno during Roman times. There have been occasional finds of Roman coins in or near the mines. A settlement at Abbey Road, just below the Great Orme, was interpreted as a miner's settlement by the excavator [5]. There is, however, a body of evidence for considerable Roman activity in the surrounding area, especially during the second to fourth centuries AD. The mineral wealth of Britannia was a prime reason for conquest. It is probable, though not proven, that there was some Roman mining at Llandudno in the area near Abbey Road, and perhaps near Gogarth. Most authorities assume that all mining then ceased until the late seventeenth century.

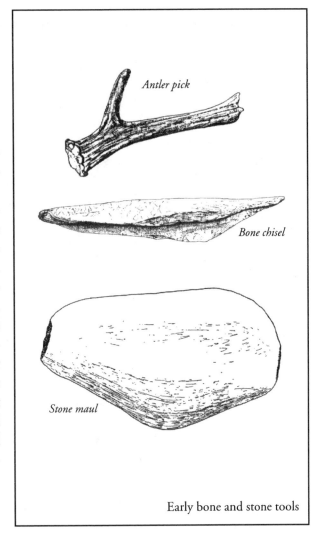

Antler pick

Bone chisel

Stone maul

Early bone and stone tools

Finds of Roman coins on the Little Orme. It has even been suggested that these low denomination coins were for paying workers in the mines.

Mining during the Industrial Revolution

The later seventeenth century heralded the start of an important era of mining activity. It was the beginning of Llandudno's Industrial Revolution. New technologies, new methods of working were introduced. These helped to crack the problems associated with working the deposits at deeper levels. The new technology allowed miners to penetrate far deeper into the harder, water-bearing lower levels. Improved smelting techniques allowed the exploitation of difficult sulphide ores. There were many setbacks. Mining seems to have been spasmodic for much of the eighteenth century, but activity gathered pace [6]. Demand was fuelled by a rise in the price of copper, by continental wars, and by the British Navy's apparently insatiable demand for copper to sheathe its warships. Copper sheathing made the ships faster and reduced the need for maintenance.

Llandudno became noted for its copper-mines. Many early travellers in Wales came to view the mines.

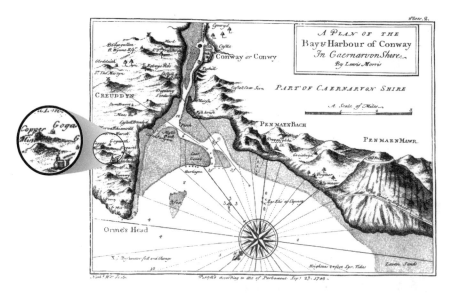

Plan of the Conwy Estuary by Lewis Morris, 1748. On the Great Orme's Head a copper-mine is marked.

'Close to the village of Llandudno is a copper-mine of considerable extent which produces nearly £2,000 of copper a year and employing upwards of 200 men. There is also another copper-mine on the heights above nearly as extensive as that adjoining the village.'

Bingley, *Excursions in North Wales*, 1804

By the nineteenth century the three important deep mines were the Old Mine, on the Bishop of Bangor's land, the New Mine, on adjacent land owned by the Mostyn Estate, both close together beside Pyllau on the Orme. Below the Orme was the more recent Tŷ Gwyn mine. Many other smaller scale levels or pits were also exploited at this time. A major engineering feat was the driving of the great Penmorfa level to de-water both the Old and New mines.

After 1850 copper-mining activity slackened. All the mines hit problems, and faced greater costs as workings had to be driven to ever deeper levels. Tŷ Gwyn was flooded out and closed in the early 1850s.

'I think that the last incident in the history of the copper-mine was the breaking in of the sea in Tŷ Gwyn mine and the miners bolting for their lives leaving their tools behind them.'

Reminiscences of John Hughes, 1917 [7]

By 1868, financial problems forced the closure of the other mines on the Great Orme itself. But by the time mining activity slackened in the mid nineteenth century Llandudno was already developing an alternative industry: tourism. After the coming of the railways into north Wales, Llandudno began to develop rapidly as a fashionable resort. After 1850, the whole focus of settlement shifted eastwards from the Great Orme itself to a new planned town, on the sandy area below the eastern cliffs (now controlled after the completion of enclosure in 1847 by the enterprising Mostyn Estate). New employment opportunities cushioned the impact of the decline of the mining industry. The Great Orme itself soon became little more than a recreational area for tourists.

Miners' and fishermen's cottages at Llandudno

A new town begins to develop below the Great Orme

5

Aspects of Mining

Prospecting

THE FIRST MINERS were probably attracted by coloured streaks of ore, visible mineralization in exposed crags, pavement and cliffs. They would have found natural faults or gulleys, or dry stream cuttings which had exposed the mineralized rock. Once a profitable area was discovered or suspected, seams could be followed. Faults and breaks in the bedding, however, could lead to a need to relocate the seams. Often there is a series of cuttings or pits sunk at intervals to follow a vein.

Early techniques of prospecting and mining for metal.
(Illustration from Agricola—a sixteenth century mining treatise)

Throughout history miners also found seams of ore bearing rock sometimes by luck, sometimes by noting small clues. Mineral rich water could ooze from a slope or rock face affecting the vegetation. Patches of dying or discoloured vegetation could also indicate areas of earlier mining. Divining techniques were sometimes used. Ploughing was sometimes important in bringing to the surface samples of ore. At Llandudno there has probably been considerable interaction between agriculture and mining. We know that in places on the Great Orme the ore lay very near to the surface, just below the turf.

The copper ore at first was found very near the surface—under the turf, as we used to say. Several such places were found in my time on the part called Bryniau Poethion.

John Hughes, a retired copper-miner speaking in 1917 [1]

Chance also played a part:

My grandfather Benjamin Edwards, Plas, had two cows which he used to put out to pasture . . . and one very wet day my father went there to fetch the cows. On the way down, one of the cows slipped and a little piece of copper was found at the place where she slipped. To the best of my recollection my father took this to Gloddaeth Hall and asked for permission to open the ground.

Recollections of John Hughes, aged 87, 1917 [2]

Later miners frequently reworked areas of former mining, or areas adjacent to those that had already been exploited, where there was a proven mass of ore-bearing rock. At Llandudno, for instance the Pyllau valley has been worked time and time again. In the nineteenth century miners worked sulphide ores from older mines or from the tips. These ores may have been been ignored by earlier generations who may have had some difficulty smelting this type of ore. Once discovered, miners followed the seams of ore wherever they led. Only in the nineteenth century was the capital and technology available to drive levels through barren rock.

The deep level after much time and heavy cost being now driven . . . gives great facilities for laying open the ground from the present workings northward on the channel of veins and flats and I should recommend it being driven from the present forebreast straight to Vivian's, the Engine Shaft, and thence northward obliquely . . . say at an angle of 30 degrees crosscutting the veins and at the same time gain a level northward by driving one fathom. . . . A level driven in this way will give great facilities in making general trials and discoveries.

Mine surveyor's report on the Old Mine in 1846 [3]

Mining techniques

The earliest mining was carried out using bone and stone tools, and by operations such as fire-setting and quenching to crack and break up the rock. Driving wedges, or pounding rock with heavy stones was another method. Evidence for all these methods has been found at Llandudno. Large quantities of charcoal have been recovered. Heavy stone mauls of sea smoothed rock, very different from the soft limestone of the headland, were brought up onto the plateau by human agency. Stone mauls leave distinctive

Firesetting in an
early mine
(Agricola)

pecked marks [4] in the rock which are very different from the marks of
metal picks or chisels. Some of the mauls discovered in the mines bear signs
of bruising on one edge. There is also some slight evidence for the use of
bronze tools.

As technology progressed iron tools gave some improvement on the bone
and stone tools used by the first miners, but in most other respects, before
the use of gunpowder, mining technology remained little changed, and the
types of ground evidence left would be similar. Even quite recent nineteenth
century prospectors used what we might class as 'primitive' mining
techniques. Some of the rows of bell pits at Bryniau Poethion (see chapter
10) are of nineteenth century origin, though the miners used a centuries old
simple mining technique of hand-excavating a shallow shaft, and throwing
up the spoil around the mouth. Excavating by hand was slow and difficult: a
matter of inches per week.

Gunpowder began to be used in Shropshire just before 1680, but its use
spread only slowly into north Wales. In the 1740s many miners were still

Sketch of the horse whimsey at Llandudno (from a plan of the abandoned mines)

using more traditional methods [5]. However, explosives, together with other new technologies, eventually enabled deeper and deeper excavations into the harder rocks of the lower layers. As mines went deeper, problems of drainage, ventilation and access had to be solved. At first water could be bucketed to the surface to keep shallow workings clear. Above the deeper shafts horse whimseys were used for winding and windmills for pumping. These were superseded by a water powered engine, and eventually by steam engines. Lack of fast flowing streams meant there was no use of waterwheels, such as we find in mines and quarries in Snowdonia. Once mining went below sea level drainage problems became even greater. (Eventually mine operators abandoned the struggle). To ventilate the mines, shutters and leather curtains could direct and control airflow to assist ventilation. The cutting of drainage or access adits at a lower level also helped. Ropes and wooden ladders allowed access into the mines, and sometimes inclined 'travelling' shafts or levels were created.

The first half of the nineteenth century saw the high water mark of copper-mining activity at Llandudno. Mining became highly capital-intensive, requiring substantial investment to pay for the engines and machinery needed to work the mines. One of the most curious of the technical developments at Llandudno was the Tom and Jerry engine installed to keep the mines free of water. It was worked by water power near the shore at Gogarth, and was linked by a line of brammock rods to pumps sited at Higher shaft near the summit. The line of hollows for the pump rods can still be traced today, and stands out visibly on aerial photographs.

The miners

Although some authors have suggested Bronze Age slave communities living in the mines, for much of the time small family groups may have worked the mines, with women and children assisting in the tasks of processing and transporting the ore. Even in the nineteenth century there is evidence that children as young as seven worked in the mine [6]. Sometimes small groups and partnerships contracted to work sections of the rock on the sort of 'bargain system' that was so familiar in the slate and stone quarries of this area. Mining could also be carried out on a 'tribute' system of payment, with a share going to the landowner or lord of the manor.

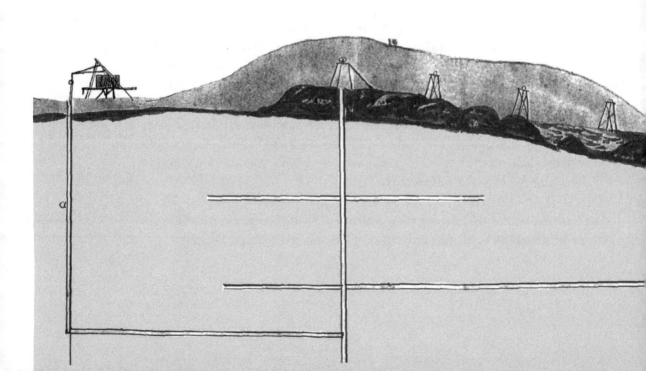

The line of the brammock
rods is an important
landscape feature that can still
be traced today

Below: engineering drawing of the buildings and machinery at Pyllau, from an abandoned mine plan [7]

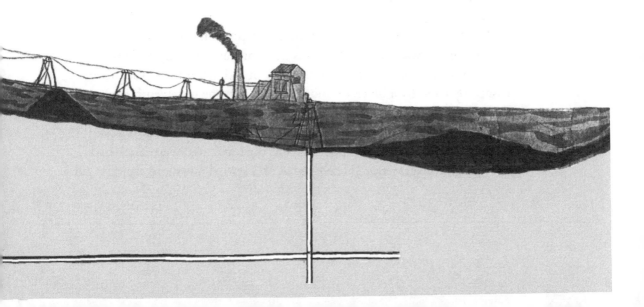

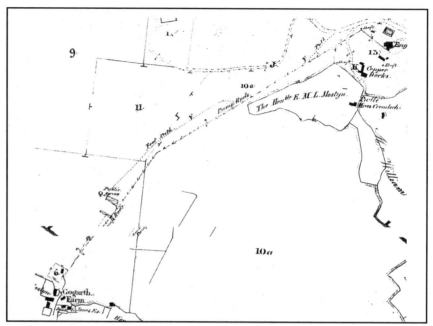

The pump rods and mine buildings are shown on the Enclosure Map of 1847

Dressing the ore

Transport of heavy ores was slow, expensive and difficult. Valuable mineral ores therefore had to be separated from waste rock. Lumps of ore bearing rock were broken up to free the ore from the surrounding rock. This initial separation of the ore was carried out underground. Hammerstones used for this purpose are found in quantities in the mines. They may have been used by miners of many periods.

Further dressing took place on the surface to concentrate the ore and separate further waste rock. This was done by hand picking and crushing. It was a job women and children could carry out. For centuries the ore was crushed by hand by a block on block process. In the nineteenth century a horse wheel was installed for this process. Next came various processes of washing, buddling or settling to carry out the separation. This process depended on the fact that copper ore and the unwanted waste rock had different specific gravities. Heavy metal ores settled out more rapidly. All

Early methods of washing and separating ore (Agricola)

this needed one important, and on the Great Orme a scarce commodity, water.

Water sources

Sources of water on this dry limestone headland would have been of great importance to the copper industry. Water was always scarce, particularly in summer. (Arthur Aiken visiting in the hot summer of 1797 recorded that all the wells on the limestone were dry). In surviving testimony by a nineteenth century miner the scarcity of water was noted [8].

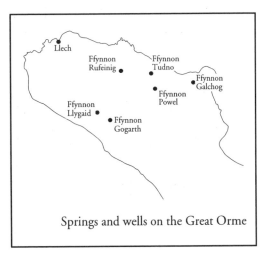

Springs and wells on the Great Orme

> The men . . . would wash it (the ore) in big tubs. Water was scarce and we had to do a lot of the work with very little water.
>
> John Hughes, ex-miner

It is no accident that there is often evidence of multi-period activity around springs and wells. At Llandudno, it has been claimed that ore was transported across to two processing sites close to water sources (Ffynnon Galchog and Ffynnon Rufeinig) for dressing [9]. Water drained from the mines, and that used for washing and processing often contained residual quantities of copper. This could be recovered either by natural settlement or by a chemical process. Copper rich water was collected in pits. Sometimes copper was recovered by an exchange process using scrap iron, with the copper being deposited on the iron as a fine powder. At Parys Mountain, Amlwch this method was developed to a great extent with batteries of precipitation pits to collect the exceptionally copper rich water. At Llandudno a different method seems to have been preferred. Water collected in what the miners referred to as *slime pits*. The heavy material was allowed to sink to the bottom, the sludge being periodically scraped out, partially dried, then sent for smelting. John Hughes, a retired copper-miner also recalled the find of an ancient washing or settling pit, very different from those in use in the nineteenth century.

> Another proof [of earlier mining] was the finding of a kind of pit or well, seven feet deep, which was full of slime and must have been used for washing copper ore. [10]
>
> John Hughes, ex-miner

Transport

Little is known about the early transport network, but one historian [11], drawing on finds of Roman coin hoards near the Little Orme, has postulated a possible routeway leading from the Great Orme, over Bryn Bia beside the Little Orme, connecting with Bryn Euryn and Dinorben hillforts. Hillforts may conceivably have had a role in the control of the early metal trade in Iron Age and Roman times. (There is a local hillfort at Pen y Dinas on the Great Orme). More pertinently, a find of Roman copper cakes was made near Dinarth on the northern side of Bryn Euryn hill fort, a location which strongly suggests that the copper came from Llandudno.

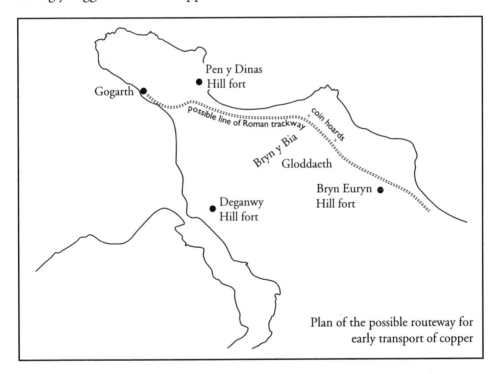

Plan of the possible routeway for early transport of copper

In the eighteenth and nineteenth century the final product was measured out by the barrow-load, and packed into bags to be transported for smelting. Its quality was sampled at the assay office to determine the payment due to the miners. Mules or ponies were used for transport, but for the larger quantities in the nineteenth century carts were also used. On the slopes these had to be braked by dragging a sled behind the cart. Transport does not seem to have been mechanized, as it was in Snowdonia, probably because the ore had to be carted only a short distance to the beach. (At Mynydd Parys too where the port was only a mile or two away horses and carts were used). In the eighteenth and nineteenth century ships called at both beaches, probably depending on the state of wind and weather, to load up with ore. John Hughes in 1917 recalled his father sending ore down to Morfa Isa for shipment. Heavy transport and shipping costs ate into much of the profit.

Smelting

It is not currently known if any early smelting was actually carried out at Llandudno. To date, no firm evidence has been found. Smelting may well have been carried out in the vicinity of Llandudno. Copper ingots of the Roman period have been found in a number of locations close by, but not to date at Llandudno itself. Two fragments of copper cakes, one bearing a Roman stamp were found at Bryn Euryn, near Colwyn Bay. John Percy a nineteenth century metallurgist also wrote in 1861 of a find of a copper cake

Some early methods of smelting (Agricola)

near Conwy. It bore a Roman inscription and weighed 22 pounds. He was convinced it had been locally smelted.

Roman copper cakes found at Bryn Euryn.

Copper carbonates can be smelted at relatively low temperatures: 985 °C is the melting point. However, sulphide ores need higher temperatures, and more complicated roasting processes to drive off the sulphur. To produce bronze, copper needs to be smelted with tin, and sometimes arsenic. Sources of tin would be in Cornwall or the lowlands of Scotland.

Very little is currently known about early smelting techniques for copper in Wales. (In contrast, early iron working has produced a considerable amount of evidence from prehistoric and Roman sites in Merioneth). Ores could be smelted using simple technologies in burning heaps or shallow pits. To reach the required temperatures a good draught is needed. Early smelting, therefore probably took place on hills, or exposed windy sites, to assist ventilation. There has been one find by an industrial archaeologist near Amlwch suggesting that ore could have been fired packed in gulleys, which would draw ventilation through them like a natural chimney [12]. Until more evidence is found, one can only speculate.

No slag has been found yet near any ancient copper-mining sites. Some authorities therefore have suggested that an early smelting process which did not produce slag is feasible[13]. High grade ores and malachites can be smelted without leaving residues. This would leave no more than a burnt stain, indistinguishable from a domestic hearth. Smelting would have required charcoal. Abundant woodland in the vicinity would have been a prerequisite. In earlier periods there would have been a far greater degree of tree cover at Llandudno. The Great Orme may once have looked rather like the wooded landscape of the Dordogne. There have been frequent finds of deer bones and antlers, and there are place name references to deer or woodland. However, by the sixteenth century the area had certainly lost most of its tree cover. Leyland's description of Caernarfonshire in 1536 records very little woodland on the Creuddyn peninsula by that time.

Much of the activity through the ages on the Great Orme involved the working of easily smelted malachite and azurite ores. These ores were being worked even as late as 1797 when Arthur Aiken, an early visitor to north Wales, mentioned *'two mines near the top of the mountain'* where two companies were employing very few men. He recorded that the miners were exploiting *'malachite or green carbonate of copper found between the limestone in strata about two inches thick.'* [14] In the more recent period copper ore was shipped to Swansea for smelting, and to Amlwch to enrich the lower grade ores mined there.

Uses for copper

Copper has a special place in history as man's earliest metal. At first copper was used alone. Later it was found that the addition of tin to make bronze, and small quantities of arsenic or other trace elements, to improve workability, produced a more durable, improved product. Throughout the prehistoric period copper was a high value, prestigious metal. Control of new technology was important in both the ordered period of the Bronze Age, and in the Iron Age. Many bronze items were for show or ceremonial use, and exhibited a high degree of craftsmanship needing many man-hours of work. In the Iron Age too, despite being superseded by the more utilitarian iron, bronze was used for ceremonial objects, heavily decorated with Celtic motifs. The Romans too coveted the metal wealth of Britannia. Roman copper cakes and stamped ingots have been found in several places in north Wales. Copper was needed for base coinage, and for a variety of utensils. Skilled craftsmen-metalworkers may have had a special place in the social

order of Celtic society. The smith was a respected craft in many early
societies. The miners themselves, primary producers of the metal, probably
had a far harder life and lower status.

Later generations needed copper for base coinage, to roof buildings or for
cisterns, and in smaller quantities for personal ornaments, buckles and pins,
horse accoutrements, as embellishment for armour, and for more mundane
domestic receptacles, and small implements. Copper throughout history has
been used for pans and utensils for both domestic use and for manufacture,
and for kettles, vats, distilling and brewing equipment etc. In the eighteenth
century war fuelled the demand for copper. In the nineteenth century
copper was important for a broad range of machinery and other products.

However, it was armaments that created the greatest use of bronze and brass.
From the reign of Edward III onwards cannon were developed for use in
warfare. (The first cannon to be deployed in north Wales were used by
Henry IV against Owain Glyndŵr's strongholds during the Glyndŵr
uprising). The development of small arms also increased demand for metal,
and by the eighteenth century the practice of sheathing warships in copper
was prevalent.

Agriculture and industry were the twin forces that have shaped the landscape
of the Orme. The last three chapters have attempted to summarise our
current state of knowledge of the history of agriculture and industry at
Llandudno. The following chapters will explore some of Llandudno's
mining and agricultural landscapes using the evidence provided by aerial
photography.

6

Two Eras of Mining at Pyllau

INDUSTRY began at Llandudno under the grey cliffs of the Pyllau valley. No place has a better claim to be the centre of copper-mining at Llandudno. Lying on a natural fault in the limestone, this is the site of the earliest known copper-mining activity of Bronze Age date in north Wales. Indeed claims have been made for this as a site of major significance for early metal mining in Europe. It was at Pyllau, too, that we find the beginnings of Llandudno's 'Industrial Revolution'. Surviving documentary evidence suggests a resurgence of mining activity on the Great Orme from the 1680s onwards, when new technology was to be employed, and shafts were to be driven to great depths [1]. What happened here in the intervening period is more shadowy. No firm evidence for Roman mining activity has been found at this spot [2]. (The area near Gogarth may be a better candidate for Roman activity). But there is some suggestion of multi-phase activity. Indeed the first extant lease for a copper-mine at Llandudno, in 1695, spoke of 'an old work in Pwlle Ray'[3] showing that the seventeenth century adventurers were well aware of earlier mining here. The place name Pyllau literally means pits and suggests that it was long recognized as an area of mining activity.

Bronze Age mining at Pyllau

The aerial photograph on the left shows Bronze Age copper workings which have recently been exposed, following the removal of over-lying spoil heaps. From the air we can get a good idea of the scale of this early mining activity. Shallow parallel trenches of the prehistoric workings are clearly visible. The

Opposite: Bronze Age mines at Pyllau

earliest miners had to excavate for ore without the benefit of metal tools. These workings are doubly impressive when one considers that mining was carried out using tools of antler, bone and stone. Charcoal finds show that firesetting was also used to assist in the process of exposing and breaking up the rock. Massive beach stones which abound on the site are believed to have been used to pound the rock to shatter it and release the ore. The grooves mark where seams of rich ore-bearing rock may have been followed and removed.

It used to be claimed that later mining always destroyed all evidence of earlier mines, but recent research has shown that this is not always the case. The early workings here were preserved, not destroyed, under later spoil. They have been exposed following extensive clearance work on the site and careful archaeological investigation of the early workings. By 1993 over 8,000 pieces of bone and nearly 1,000 hammerstones had been found in the workings, along with charcoal, and some small fragments of bronze. Early trenching on the vein was superseded by open cast working, and later by mining at depth. Signs of Bronze Age mining activity are claimed to have been found down to a depth of 70 metres, covering an area in excess of 24,000 square metres [4]. Some claims for Bronze Age mining in Wales and Ireland have generated heated debate. Nevertheless, the weight of evidence now accumulated, does seem to confirm Bronze Age mining activity here. Ten radio-carbon dates (obtained from various sealed locations both on the surface and at depth) suggest mining activity here in the period 1800–500 BC. The earliest dates were from surface workings. Supposed tools have been matched to actual gouges in the roof or walls in some cases, for instance. Wear marks have been noted on many stones and distinctive pecked marks caused by pounding with heavy stones have been found on walls and roofs.

Close by, beyond the bottom part of the aerial photograph, lie the remains of the neolithic burial chamber of Llety'r Filiast. The proximity of the two sites hints at immense cultural and economic change between the Neolithic and Bronze Age periods. The area was transformed from a sacred place of tribal and ritual importance to an industrial site. We can only guess at the conflict of cultures and the enormity of the changes that must have occurred.

Mining during the industrial revolution

The photograph on the following page shows the Pyllau copper-mining site from the opposite direction looking south. The shed which is in the top right of the photograph on page 50, lies at the bottom of the second picture. The landscape is under snow cover and despite the overcast skies, the conditions significantly enhance the amount of information that aerial photography can provide.

There was considerable copper-mining activity at Llandudno in the later eighteenth century and up to the mid-nineteenth century when Llandudno began to develop as a resort. Much of the spoil visible is from deep mining of this period, and consists of the waste and mining debris thrown up around access shafts. The lunar-like landscapes left by mining are not easy to interpret at the best of times, and they can be even more confusing when they result from several different phases of activity on the same site. In this case, however, both documentary evidence from the archives and oral testimony may provide a key to help interpret some of the more recent elements. There is surviving map evidence from the 1840s showing the location of the deep mines and shafts of the industrial mining period. Both the tithe map of 1840 and the enclosure map of 1847, produced when the mines were still working, show shafts, buildings and trackways. It is possible to correlate some of this evidence with the relict features visible on aerial photographs. Also extremely helpful is an oral account by a retired miner published in a local newspaper of 1917 [7]. He began work (at the age of seven and a half) at the copper-mines in 1837, and his testimony provides an eye-witness account of the

Mine buildings at the Old Mine at Pyllau. (Engineer's drawing)

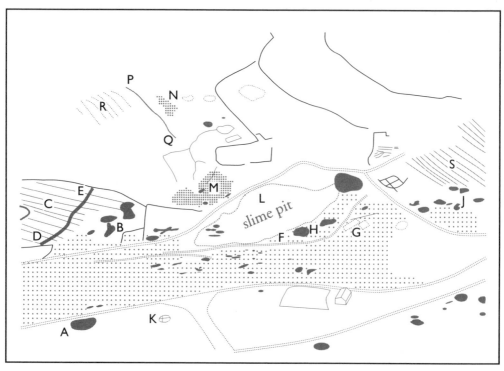

Llandudno mines at the height of their exploitation in the nineteenth century. Many of the features on this aerial photograph correlate very closely with his evidence, despite the considerable demolition and clearance that is known to have taken place in the 1950s.

'The shafts of the old mine were known as the Middle Shaft (the engine shaft) and Shaft Uwch. There was another on the south side of the Middle Shaft near the slime pool. . . . A fourth shaft was situate on Bryniau Poethion and a fifth just outside Pyllau farm . . . I have told you about pools holding slime. Well there was one rather big one reaching from Maes y Facrell field towards the shaft of the Old Mine which was fully 50 yards wide. My father Joseph Hughes of the King William (a public house) used to sell the slime from that for 15s a ton.'

Evidence of John Hughes, a former miner speaking in 1917

Many shafts and craters are visible, highlighted by the snow cover. There is one at A almost under the road and another at B directly in line in the centre of the photograph. This lies on top of ridge and furrow ploughing, C which in turn overlies an ancient bank, running from D to E, dividing the Maes y Facrell field in two. In the centre of the picture, there is a large area of spoil and pits and various other features which form the core of the Old Mine complex. Amongst the spoil rectangular foundations of some former mine buildings are faintly visible at F and G. On the site were storage sheds to hold the ore, cabins, a smithy, foundry and assay office (where samples from the ore were tested to determine the copper content). Beside Vivian's shaft, at H stood the engine house which kept the deeper shafts and workings free of water. Only one shaft is noted on the earlier Ordnance Survey maps on the land adjacent to Pyllau farm, but from the air there is evidence of extensive activity. A series of pits and depressions including a large shaft are visible, at J, beyond the road leading to Pyllau farm, and a few just at the bottom of the field inside the enclosed farmland. Close beside the farmhouse was the main

Opposite: copper-mining area at Pyllau

shaft for the New Mine, and two other workings. A circular feature at K with an interesting cross-shaped feature inside it, beside the first shaft mentioned (at A), may also be connected with the mining.

The large crater-like depression L would appear to be the 'pit of slime' referred to by miner John Hughes. This was used for the secondary recovery of copper from the washings from ore processing, and perhaps from water drained out of the mine by the pumping engine. The Bronze Age workings are not visible in this earlier aerial photograph. They lie buried under eighteenth and nineteenth century spoil. A road crosses near the site where they lie buried.

We get little indication from surface evidence visible here of the great depth or extent of the underground mines at Pyllau. The waste on the surface is only a fraction of the total waste actually produced, and is mainly spoil from excavating the deep shafts and debris from dressing the ore. Waste from the network of levels, galleries and shafts was usually left underground. From the excavations here it is known that underground Bronze Age galleries were back-filled at this site [8]. Back-filling by early miners can be differentiated, as it is cemented together. Miners of the Industrial Age also back-filled old caverns, often in the process sealing and preserving earlier deposits of bone and charcoal. Before they were cleared, plentiful samples of blue/green copper ores could be picked up off the tips in this area. Quantities of hammerstones and copper stained bone were also to be found around the spoil heaps.

On the slopes above the Pyllau valley at M and N are other areas of what seems to be spoil and debris, which probably represent some earlier mining or prospecting. There is also a possible trench running from P to Q. Some other marks are in fact the strata of the limestone showing through the snow cover. These are on a different alignment to the rig and furrow.

Evidence of earlier agriculture

Despite the fact that this is an industrial site, the aerial photograph also offers incidental evidence of earlier agriculture. Around the fringes of the mined area traces of relict agricultural landscapes are visible. Industrial evidence overlies traces of farming at this site. The ridge and furrow at C, pre-dating the eighteenth and nineteenth century mining activity, has already been mentioned. This probably represents some of the narrow strips of the medieval township of Yr Wyddfid. Mining activity has devastated the farmland of this valley. Across the valley, at R, in a large field on the hill are further traces of what may be faint earlier, weathered cultivation ridges (or perhaps trenches?), seemingly on a different alignment to lines of limestone strata which are also visible. These are overlain in part by debris. The small irregular enclosures on these slopes may also stand on more ancient footings than many of the other field boundaries visible here, and may relate to some pastoral activity. In the fields belong to Pyllau farm at S, rig and furrow, runs across the valley (on the same alignment as the ancient cultivation already noted). There are many other intriguing features, but there is not scope to discuss them here.

To make sense of these features, the craters, pits, spoil, and traces of cultivation, we need to think in terms of a series of superimposed landscapes representing activity by groups of people who lived at different times. A lot is known now about the Bronze Age mines and the eighteenth and nineteenth century activity, but around these points in time are other 'layers' of human activity for which faint traces in the landscape remain. Aerial photography can provide a surprising amount of information, despite the highly damaged nature of the industrial remains. What we see in the snow photograph had already been subject to demolition and clearance work in the 1950s. The central area was totally cleared in the late 1980s. Spoilheaps of the industrial period were mechanically removed.

7

Early Agriculture and Industry at Hwylfa'r Ceirw

DESERTED fields on a lonely plateau tell their own eloquent story of human activity and abandonment. In the next photograph we move from the Pyllau valley to the north west of the Great Orme. Here there is a most remarkable area of surviving early landscape. At Pyllau, it was possible to use findings from excavation, archive material and oral testimony to explain some, though not all, of the surviving landscape features. The Hwylfa'r Ceirw area is far less well documented. Most nineteenth century maps for instance show only a blank area here. Now we must rely on the landscape evidence alone. The photograph opposite will amply repay detailed examination. It offers valuable evidence both about early agriculture, and about small scale mining activity. By examining carefully the relationships between different features on the site, we can piece together from the landscape evidence the story of several phases of human activity here.

The stone alignment

The main feature for which the area is noted is a 'stone alignment', running from the edge of a rectangular enclosure to a cleft in the cliff. It runs beside two large stones on the western edge of a former rectangular enclosure. It may be earlier than some of the cultivation visible. The function of these stones is not fully understood. This may be a monument of ritual significance (a sort of processional avenue), or it may be little more than a lane or drove way bounded by double banks, perhaps forming part of some

Opposite: abandoned field systems at Hwylfa'r Ceirw

The Stone Alignment

'On the same side are the remains of several rude walls without mortar called Llety Fadog . . . and not far from it is a strait narrow path, with stones on each side, probably the remains of two walls; a watch place for Deer as the name Gwylfa y Ceirw signifies.'

Thomas Pennant,
Tours in Wales, 1777.

'Not far from the church are two rows of upright stones called Hwylfa'r Ceirw, the High Road of the Deer. Tradition says of these, that it was a path by which the deer, which once abounded in the mountains of Caernarvonshire, used to descend to a meadow below, long since covered by the sea. This explanation is extremely absurd, and, till some better is found, we must rest in ignorance both as to their origin and use.'

Rev W. Bingley, *A Tour of North Wales,* 1804.

early system of land division. It stops at the cliff edge. Local legend, however, has a more colourful interpretation. The placename *Hwylfa'r Ceirw,* literally means *the roadway of the deer.* The stone alignment has long exercised a fascination on antiquarians and early travellers in north Wales.

The agricultural evidence

On aerial photographs, however, the most striking feature is the area of former fields and cultivation. This early landscape at Hwylfa'r Ceirw lies outside the present day farmed area. There is clear evidence of many periods of activity. A network of interlocking terraces and plots, bearing clear traces of former cultivation, is visible. The area has been photographed from different angles and heights, under a range of lighting and weather conditions. The analysis that follows is a result of combining information from a number of sorties, made under different conditions of lighting and weather. It is the oblique aerial shots, in particular that frequently provide particularly detailed archaeological information. We are now going to see how much we can discover about activity at this site, simply by analysing a range of aerial photography.

Agriculture here at one time was organized within a system of small, mainly rectangular fields. These neat plots are almost certainly spade dug. In one place at A they can be seen forking round a boulder. There is a possibility too that the terraced plots may have evolved from some earlier system. This may have been a core area of permanent cultivation, worked and reworked over a long period. At B the cultivation ridges can be seen overlying an earlier field bank; nearby later cultivation seems to have broken down an earlier terrace. At C a later rectangular enclosure seems to have been laid out over an earlier field system. There may even be two 'ages' of cultivation ridges here. In one place at D later cultivation overlies earlier rig and furrow. On rougher ground at E are traces of more weathered ridges, with the ridges on the same alignment as this earlier cultivation. The slightly differing alignments of the blocks of cultivation ridges suggest strongly that this is a multi-period landscape. A circular feature in one of the enclosures may be a hut site or some other structure (excavation would be needed to confirm its nature). There are other boundaries or banks, including a D shaped

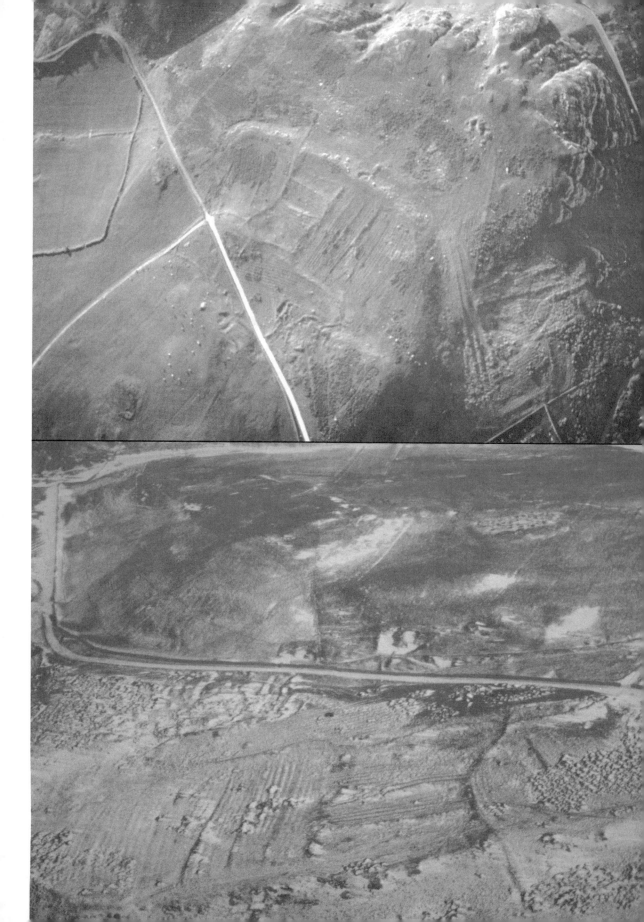

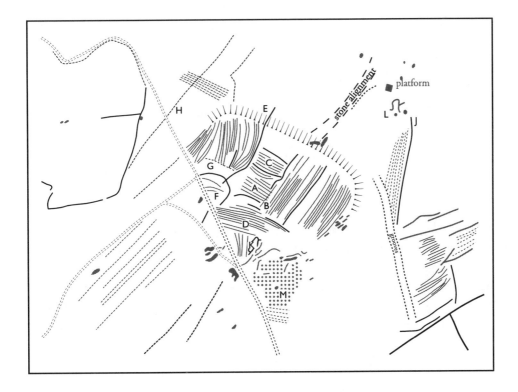

enclosure at F which has cultivation inside it. One field boundary at G is marked by a line of stones. There are indications that agricultural activity once spread over a far wider area beyond the field system. In addition to the field terraces and plots, there are vestiges of more extensive arable cultivation on rougher outlying ground, for instance at H. This is somewhat different in character and degree of weathering to the adjacent cultivation. It may represent some form of outfield cultivation, or the evidence may be pointing to a contraction of arable cultivation here. It is also clear on other aerial photographs, that the terraced field system once extended right to the cliff top. The right angled corners of a former field bank can be seen at J and there is a similar bank lower down the hill. The area they enclose bears traces of cultivation. A building or house site at K shows as a rectangular feature. Pennant calls these ruins Llety Fadog, and one 1849 source [2] describes them as the former residence of Prince Madog, (although another source, a map of 1861, locates Llety Fadog within the present farmland of

Opposite top: vertical view of Hwylfa'r Ceirw. Many other intriguing features are visible. Below: snow cover highlights the traces of arable cultivation, which extend onto even more marginal ground

Parc [1]). The structure at ᴋ cuts into an area of earlier cultivation. Its entrance has been blocked by later spoil. There are also faint traces of a circular enclosure visible from certain angles.

Small scale mining activity

Intermingled with the plots and terraces is unmistakable evidence of small scale mining activity. Several areas of small scale cuttings, spoil heaps, disturbed ground, and what may be work floors or processing areas can be distinguished. Near the cliff beside ᴊ are further mine spoil heaps from a small scale working. (One even wonders if some of the linear scars may represent channelling of surface water to scour and expose some of the slopes, as several lead to gulleys). In places there are several pits or cuts in line, where a seam or outcrop of ore has been followed. The surface indications suggest small scale mining activity, perhaps just working exposed outcrops or ore close to the surface. Sometimes, however, workings can be more extensive than the surface evidence suggests. There has also been some exploitation of seams outcropping in the crags on the steeper slopes below. In one small scale working or trial, a low entrance leads to a hole in the floor which drops down into a level. There is an adit in Badger's cave above Marine Drive [2]. There are traces of mining at Hafnant, just to the west.

Possible ore-processing site beside Ffynnon Rufeinig

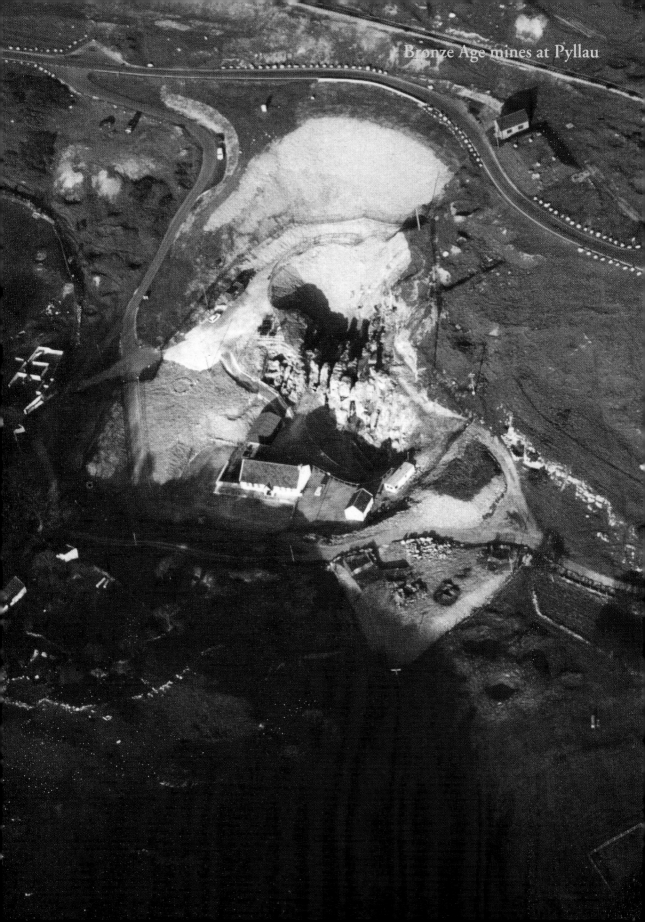

Bronze Age mines at Pyllau

Pyllau industrial
landscape

Mynydd Isaf

medieval fields on the common

Mining landscape,
Bryniau Poethion

This is small scale surface activity, very different in character from the more extensive deep eighteenth and nineteenth century workings further east. This type of 'subsistence' mining would be consistent with a suggestion of part time mining/farming activity. There may be multi-period mining activity. In places mining activity overlies or intermingles closely with the cultivated plots. In one area mining debris can be seen overlying ridges of the arable cultivation. The interaction between farming and mining activity on this site is extremely interesting. It is even conceivable that in this area, the arable cultivation and some of the small scale mining activity could be interconnected. Ploughing activity sometimes brought to light samples of minerals lying close to the surface.

Ore processing

There is a water source nearby, the spring of Ffynnon Rufeinig, shown opposite. It is claimed that this was one of two wells on the Great Orme, used for washing and processing the copper ore [3]. In 1909, at a time when many ex-miners were still living, this was noted as a former ore processing

Behind these runs a spring of beautiful water, but the ground from which it runs has been lately cut up; an ineffectual effort having been made to convert the water to the uses of one of the mines [4]

Washing of ores in buddles or wooden troughs (Agricola)

site, probably one that had been utilized for long periods. There is other evidence for, at least, nineteenth century processing activity here. The account written in 1849 probably refers to this spring [3]. Certainly the area of debris and disturbed ground nearby could well be indicating a former ore processing area. Sections of walling could be structures connected with the ore processing. The evidence of a faint line of depressions running down from the well area might even indicate the site of a possible series of chutes, troughs or buddling boards for washing the ore. Several small finger dumps are faintly visible. The last activity on the site occurred in the 1900s when the Urban District Council carried out some work at Ffynnon Rufeinig to harness this source to supply the cemetery, before mains water reached the area [4.] Some debris may be attributable to this.

Many of the features discussed here may be best interpreted in terms of a number of different superimposed landscapes. The way in which industrial activity has encroached on the agricultural area is also noteworthy. Although this is a small area, it contains a surprising amount of evidence about landscape change over time.

Why has this evidence survived? The ancient landscape has escaped obliteration because it is well outside the modern farmed areas. Indeed evidence from tithe and enclosure maps show it was well outside of the nineteenth century farmed areas too. In the green improved farmland and pasture land of the post-enclosure farm to the east very little survives. Only very faint lines and depressions suggest possible activity. There are several testimonies from early nineteenth century writers suggesting that this area had been long deserted.

> 'The old Manse lies a little left of the Church . . . To the right there is the farm of Dolfechan, and these are the only places on that side of the mountain which are now cultivated'. [5]

Many late eighteenth and nineteenth century writers commented on the bleak, windswept landscape in this area. In view of its exposed position, the evidence for so much intensive arable cultivation is rather surprising. It has probably always been rather marginal land.

8

Open Field Farming, Settlement and Mining near Saint Tudno's Church

ONCE, labouring ox teams dragged the heavy plough through the furrow. Now sheep nibble the tight knit turf, and tourists picnic or unthinkingly park their cars on the common. Traces of ridge and furrow on the open common tell us that this land was once ploughed. On the photograph overleaf a system of fields deeply marked with ridges from arable cultivation is visible. At the head of the system the remains of a number of rectangular structures can be seen; these may well be associated with the field system. The fields lie outside of the modern cultivated area, on the common running down to Saint Tudno's Church. This explains their survival. They have not been damaged by modern agriculture or deep ploughing. The area is divided by low walls or baulks.

How were these ridges formed? There are clues in their pattern. The broad slightly curving ridges are the result of repeatedly ploughing the land in a particular way, and probably took centuries to form [1]. The plough turned the sods in one direction on the outward leg and facing the opposite way on the return leg, so that the two ridges lay together forming an inverted V. Later ridges were formed in parallel. Over time this created a broad backed ridge whose traces are still visible today. When the entire system is viewed from the air it can be seen that some strips curve slightly at the end in the form of a reversed S, a result of the turning of the ox team. Some of the more extreme curves, however, also reflect the effect of changes in levels in the slope, which resulted in the uneven pattern.

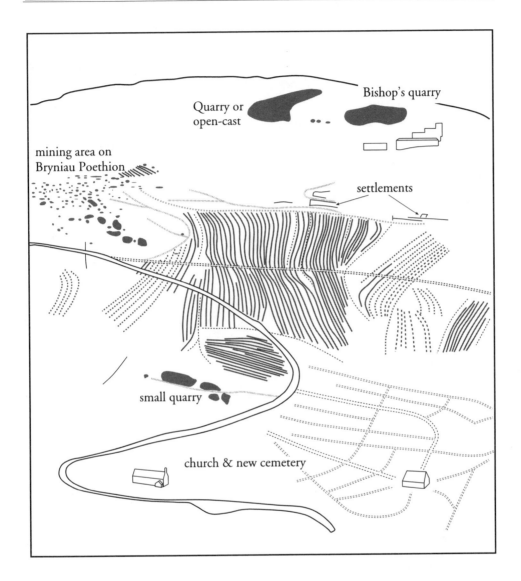

Quarry or open-cast

Bishop's quarry

mining area on Bryniau Poethion

settlements

small quarry

church & new cemetery

These fields are significantly broader than the neat, spade-dug, linear plots noted at Hwylfa'r Ceirw in the previous chapter, about three times as wide. From the ground evidence we can infer that cultivation using a team of oxen was practised here. Most of the ridge and furrow is of uniform width. However, in certain oddly shaped areas, wider ridges can be seen. These may have been ploughed after the work on the longer fields was completed, or even dug by hand because of the awkward shape of the remaining plot. The

Opposite: field system on the common

surviving pattern of plots at the right hand side however suggests that these fields could have superseded some earlier arrangement. The system probably originated in the later medieval period. It seems to represent the spread of new settlers or farming practices at Llandudno. Two sites or settlements with remains of buildings lie below the summit. One is a platform house, built on an artificially levelled platform, with a distinctive drainage hood, a type common in the fourteenth or fifteenth century [2].

This field system probably extended further east into what is now enclosed farmland. Some evidence has been obliterated by modern farming practices, but according to the 1840 tithe map, within the nearby farm of Penmynydd

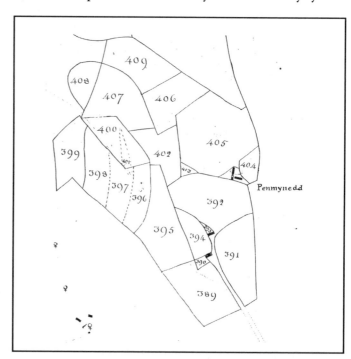

The 1840 tithe map showing parallel fields at Penmynydd Isaf divided only by low baulks.

Isaf, a last fragment of a system of fields separated by low banks still survived in 1840. The system on the common had by then gone out of use (probably several centuries earlier) allowing the land to revert to common grazing, for the tithe map of 1840 shows large areas of the Orme as unenclosed common. Even inside the enclosed farmland of the fields belonging to Penmynydd Isaf, the earlier system has left an imprint. Some of the awkward, jagged field boundaries that can still be seen today hold clues. The complicated field pattern visible there today reflects a number of influences. Certain boundaries align with the relict fields on the common. Others are on different alignments, some aligning with the path or track, running direct from Penmynydd Uchaf towards the church.

There is an account written in 1849, before there had been time for any post-Enclosure Act land improvements, which suggests that several parts of the Great Orme at that time still bore traces of prominent cultivation ridges:

> From the manner in which many of the more sheltered patches appear to have been laid out in ridges, there is little doubt the greater part of the mountain top was at one time in a state of cultivation. But now, with a slight exception, the sheep feed and roam over it at will. [3]

The church and its environs

To the north of the common lies the parish church of Llandudno. Saint Tudno's Church is believed to be an early foundation, ascribed to the sixth century. The earliest masonry is of eleventh or twelfth century date, but traces of an earlier wooden church were found in the floor [4]. From the air the church itself appears to sit inside what seems to be a rectangular enclosure or earthwork. Two corners and sides can be traced, including a section of walling below the church. A crop mark of what may be an annexe is visible in drought conditions,

The church appears to lie within a rectangular earthwork

Saint Tudno's Church

It stands alone on an elevated and extensive plain, just above the sea, in the very seat of desolation and bareness; exposed to every wind that blows; destitute even of a single tree to shelter or protect it. I could not distinguish a hut or cottage in the neighbourhood.

Bingley *A Tour of North Wales*, 1804

The church is exposed from the bleakness of its situation to violent gales in winter and it is far removed from any dwelling.

Williams *History of Aberconway*, 1835

below the wall. Other sections have been destroyed by the creation of the new cemetery.

By the eighteenth century the focus of settlement and activity had long shifted much further east, and the church stood in isolation, apart from its rectory, Dolfechan, and a small enclosed patch of glebe land. When it was unroofed in a storm in 1839, the church remained derelict until 1855. The new Victorian cemetery area adjacent was constructed in 1859. But however desolate the picture painted by the antiquarians of the eighteenth century, evidence visible on aerial photographs suggests there has been human activity in the immediate area at some time in the past, (although, of course, aerial photographs alone cannot date the remains). Directly south of the church is an area of cultivation respected by the fields on the common inside a surviving section of an ancient enclosing bank. It might conceivably be something related to the church just below.

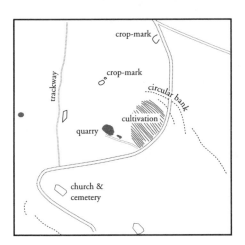 

On the hill immediately to the west of the former rectory and new cemetery can be seen vestiges of terraces and some small field plots. Below the church faint vestiges of narrow strips are also visible in very dry weather conditions. The small plots may have some affinity with the Hwylfa'r Ceirw complex on the plateau just above described in the previous chapter. It may be that these systems of short terraced or rectangular plots indicate Dark Age (early medieval) farming and the fields on the common, discussed above, a later medieval system. Whatever date the features may be, they indicate quite intensive human activity in the area near to the church. Far from being a setting of monastic isolation, the church must have been a focus for the people who cultivated these fields. The surviving traces raise many questions.

Remains of industry

Close scrutiny of the aerial photographs also reveals traces of small scale industry in the vicinity of the church. There is a small, fairly recent, quarried area visible close to the church on the slope above. Below the churchyard, is an area of spoil from small scale working or from prospecting activity. Hidden in trees and scrub on the slope to the south east of the church is the site of an old level, which was noted on the Llandudno Enclosure map of

1847 [5]. The way the field boundaries go around the area suggests that it could be a working whose origins could pre-date the enclosed fields. One wonders too if there has ever been prospecting or mining activity in the vicinity of the church? The new Victorian cemetery has obliterated some evidence, for Edmund Hyde Hall in 1809 mentioned two graves to the south of the church but outside the consecrated area, reputed by local folklore to be the graves of a giant and a giantess [6]. Could these have been spoilheaps? There are other traces of spoil in gulleys under the cemetery wall. This area is on the line of the most productive north to south copper bearing lodes, running northwards from the Pyllau valley. It must have attracted the attention of prospectors.

Running downhill from the Hwylfa'r Ceirw area are broad, parallel grooves, gouging the hillside. They may predate the new cemetery. Although they follow lines of natural limestone terraces, the way they cut earlier field boundaries and cultivation suggests they are the result of some human agency. Their function is not fully understood at present [7], but they may relate to some industrial purpose.

People have farmed and worked in this part of the Great Orme in the past. They have left their traces etched in the landscape. This is a very 'busy' landscape. The earthwork evidence, contrasts strongly with the isolation and desolation suggested by the descriptions of the eighteenth and early nineteenth century travellers.

Traces of plots and terraces, and grooves in the steep hillside

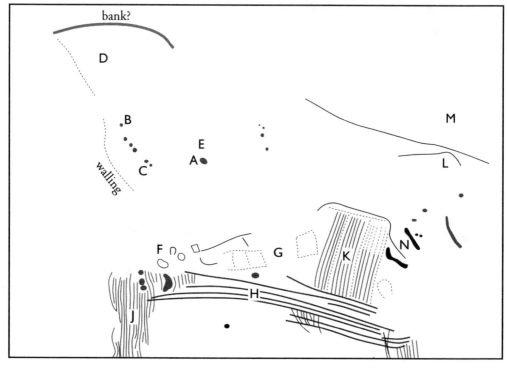

bank?

D

B

E

A

C

walling

M

L

F

G

K

N

H

J

9

Agriculture, Settlement and Mining near Mynydd Isaf

T HE STUDY of the past is often an exercise in detective work. It involves examination of small clues, and faint remains. There is certainly little enough to be seen around Mynydd Isaf today by the occasional tourist who ventures over there. However, landscape evidence has survived here for settlement, arable agriculture and an interesting area of small scale mining activity. The focus of this present chapter will be to examine in detail some of the surface landscape evidence, using aerial photography.

Mynydd Isaf itself is a low limestone plateau, affording excellent views, scarped most of the way round. It lies on the northeastern edge of the Great Orme. Immediately to the south west the land has been enclosed and improved. Nearby, a shaft was revealed during the 1993 floods, and there is a vein running north towards Porth Helyg. Many intriguing features are visible on the plateau. Traces of walling on the scarp edge exist in places, and there is just a suggestion of a possible bank, at the back where the natural scarp gives out. At least one pit A can be seen clearly. From the air small, faint circles are visible . Some may be a line of small bell pits B–C (later filled in), though the possibility of natural sink holes must also be considered. A faint cropmark enclosure D on the plateau may indicate some early settlement or activity here. In drought conditions there are even faint suggestions of parallel land divisions E on part of the plateau. The small natural knoll is known as *Gorsedd Isaf.* Below the plateau, an area of ground, covered in bracken and rough grass lies outside of the present day farmed area. A most remarkable area of early landscape exists here.

Opposite: agriculture and settlement below Mynydd Isaf

Settlement and agriculture below Mynydd Isaf

Clear evidence of settlement is visible at the base of Mynydd Isaf. Four rectangular structures (long huts) F appear to be in line, two lying against an ancient bank. This bank overlies other small banks which seem to make up a system of very small square enclosures G, in one of which a number of small circles appear. It has been suggested that these could be small bell pits, or something connected with ore processing, though there are other possible interpretations (for instance habitation sites?) which only excavation could resolve. In the same area part of an elongated enclosure can be seen.

In addition to the series of very small enclosures already noted, there is abundant evidence of former arable cultivation, despite the fact that this is a 'marginal' area, outside the present day enclosed farmland. One long strip H can be seen. Its reversed S curve suggests it was plough-formed. It overlies other traces of cultivation J and K where narrower ridges run in a different direction. On one side these seem to be divided by banks into a series of linear plots at K, rather reminiscent of the Hwylfa'r Ceirw plots, and there is a trace of a field bank around them to the south west. A similar parallel bank L can be seen further west still. This does look like the remains of an early field system organized on a linear basis. The cultivation traces visible here seem to represent two different phases of agricultural activity on this site, for the ridges are of different widths and on the left there is a definite area of cross ploughing. Here it can be seen that plough marks from the long strips overlie the ridges from the shorter field system. This apparently obscure area offers us valuable dating evidence, therefore, which may also help to sequence the field systems discussed in the previous two chapters.

Mining activity

Small cuts and isolated scatters of debris suggest possible very small scale prospecting or mining or ore processing near the settlement area and possibly around the base of Mynydd Isaf itself.

Bell pits and early mining
above Porth Helyg

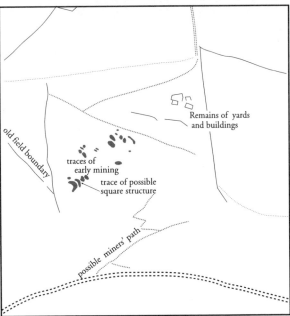

Plot of the early mining
area

In the adjacent field above Porth Helyg at M where the hillside steepens, there is a heavily weathered looking complex of small pits debris and spoil. From their size and weathered appearance they may indicate early mining or associated activity. The spoil heaps form two groups. In the lower cluster, a square structure is faintly visible on infra red aerial photographs, though not discernible in normal light. Two distinct bell pits are discernible in the upper group. In other places the spoil is in a confused series of heaps. This may possibly indicate a reworking of the tips by later prospectors. Reworking of old mining areas was a common practice. Later miners often found that earlier miners had ignored the sulphide ores (which require complex smelting processes), and were often able to recover considerable quantities of copper ore from old tips. Spoil and disturbed ground extend further down the steep slope. There are two small faint square features which may be of significance. It seems that here is some small scale mining site. A zigzag path descending the steep slope is probably a miners' path. Miners were well acquainted with the local geography of cliffs and slopes. Above the bell pits, also in the rough ground, is a complex of rectangular structures, which may or may not be associated with mining activity.

A trial trench excavation was made here in 1990. Animal bones and teeth heavily impregnated with copper were found in the vicinity. Excavation confirmed the presence of graded debris, not dissimilar to that found near Pyllau. It is a potential site for early ore processing. It was claimed the tips were reworked in the early 1800s.

In the cliffs below not visible in these photographs is a man-made mine trial from the industrial period.In the nineteenth century a level was driven along a spring line, towards the Penmorfa level. This suggests that there were promising indications of seams of ore in this area, which earlier prospectors may also have noted.

Ore processing?

Below Mynydd Isaf is an important water source N, the lime-rich waters of Ffynnon Galchog, a petrifying spring that left objects placed in it encrusted with calcite. A black gash can be seen below the field terraces. There may even be leats leading from it towards the cliff. A trackway can be traced leading down towards the well. A small square rectangular feature faintly visible in some photographs is probably associated with the well site. To the east is a faint line of a wall. The ground around the spring is very wet. It has been claimed that this water source was used for dressing copper ores. Tradition claimed this as a Roman ore processing site. An account of 1909 mentions the spring as

> '. . one of the two places on the Great Orme used by the old miners (and probably the Romans) for the purpose of washing the copper ore from the mines.' [2]

Ores are said to have been transported here for processing. There is little sign of debris or substantial mounds in the actual vicinity of the well area, except one fan-shaped mound. Early twentieth century writers, however, suggested that clearances had occurred here and that much of Marine Drive, the Victorian carriageway around the Orme, had been surfaced with gravels carted away from the ore processing area [3].

Finds of a Bronze Age hoard in a cleft below confirm that this was an area of early human activity at Llandudno [4].

This is an interesting area of surviving historic landscape, showing evidence of multi-period activity. It has survived because of its location on extremely marginal land. Much of the settlement and agricultural evidence may be of Dark Age and later medieval date, though other relict traces may relate to earlier activity. At least two phases of agriculture are represented, and the superimposed cultivation areas are extremely useful in offering a sequence, which may help to illuminate other relict landscape on the Great Orme. The landscape evidence itself tells a story of different groups of people using this site in different ways for both agricultural and industrial purposes.

10

Mining Landscapes at Bryniau Poethion

JUST TO the east of the Great Orme summit, on the common, lies one of the most remarkable mining landscapes in north Wales. This series of bell pits and other traces of mining are traditionally regarded as the result of what has been called 'the Welsh California'. This was Llandudno's equivalent of the Gold Rush, but with copper rather than gold as its objective. Around 1849 there was a frenzy of prospecting and mining by small groups of independent copper-miners, most of them using primitive mining techniques more reminiscent of an earlier age [1]. Previous writers have suggested that no prospecting for metals was carried out on Bryniau Poethion until the nineteenth century.

Some of the scars and bell pits visible here probably relate to nineteenth century activity. But from the air there are some suggestions that we are looking here at a more complex landscape and a closer investigation reveals a number of significant factors which suggest the mining is not all of a single type. Several techniques of mining can be distinguished. There are numerous small bell pits.

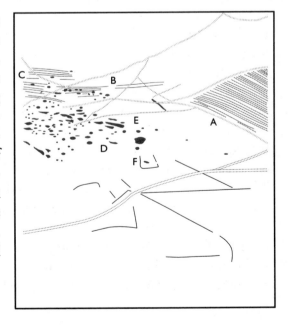

Opposite: bell pits and other remains of copper-mining on Bryniau Poethion

In the ascent, the ancient copper-mines and those of more recent date must not be forgotten. One of the oldest has been worked since the time of the Romans and the yield of ore has been immense. At the present time the land is let off in small allotments to the miners who call the mountain 'Welsh California'. Three or four of these take a lot and immediately sink a shaft for the purpose of digging out the ore. Upon the amount realized they have to pay a royalty to the owner. The hill is laid open with nearly a hundred of these cuttings. Some of the men have netted large amounts by these speculations. Others have worked for months without meeting with a profitable vein. This under ordinary circumstances would be very disheartening, but the men are industrious and engage in the two-fold occupation of miner-fishermen. They keep themselves above want and labour at their diggings with great diligence. [2]

These circular doughnut-shaped features with a central depression, represent the remains of shallow pits, dug by hand and entered by crude ladders. Once the area underneath was hollowed out to a certain size, the pit was usually abandoned and another pit sunk near by. Many of the pits are in lines, either because they follow a productive seam, or because of the way the 'bargains' were allocated in the 1849 frenzy of mining activity. Not all the pits are of the same age. A few bell pits seem quite weathered. Some may only be easily visible from the air. Occasionally a pit overlies an earlier working or other debris. In one extensive area mining has been carried out in trenches (one even wonders if there are two phases of activity, with very ancient trenches being re-opened by the mid nineteenth century miners?). There is also a scarred area of larger pits and deep shafts. These different ways of working may indicate separate phases of mining activity.

Evidence from underground investigations carried out in 1967 and 1968 helps to illuminate the different types of mining activity here. Members of Shropshire Mining Society, using caving techniques, explored several shafts under Bryniau Poethion. Their report and some artefacts collected are held in the County Archives [3]. Their investigations confirmed several different types of working below the surface. Nineteenth century artefacts were found (including a newspaper!), also numerous hammerstones which could possibly be of an earlier date. Some shafts were 'very shallow'. A deeper shaft opened out at 100 feet, with 'cavernous workings' leading from the shaft. A very deep nineteenth century shaft (followed down to 400 feet) was located at the surface and at several points below ground. It was described as being 'very dangerous', with flooding at the lower levels. Other 'large cavernous workings' were noted. These different types of workings may well be indicating different phases of exploitation. Later excavations in the later 1980s by the Great Orme Exploration Society, also confirmed the variety of types of mining under Bryniau Poethion [4]. Many of the shafts and workings under Bryniau Poethion interconnected, suggesting that some earlier workings, could have been used as access ways. Severe flooding and torrential rain in March 1993 caused several pits on Bryniau Poethion to collapse inwards, producing further evidence of far more substantial workings than were previously supposed. It is possible that some pits may be pre-nineteenth century. That there was at least some pre 1849 activity is suggested by a reference in a document of 1783 to 'the company in the common' [5]. However, there may be remains of much earlier workings.

In places on the hill lie traces of an earlier agricultural landscape. Corrugations of broad cultivation ridges can be seen. Cultivation seems to have been quite extensive. Previous writers who have noted these traces of cultivation have tended to class all ridge and furrow as *medieval*. From the air, however, it is possible to distinguish three 'ages' of cultivation ridges on Bryniau Poethion. Only in one small area (at A) do the bell pits and mining debris overlie the sharply delineated cultivation ridges that belong to the later medieval field system on the common discussed earlier in chapter 8. Over other parts of the hillside ridges are less crisp, broader and more weathered. Near the base of the hill (at B) the ridges are very faint. They may even be prehistoric. The existence of a round hut on Bryniau Poethion [6] might also imply a prehistoric date for one area of cultivation. Certainly they seem to represent an agricultural phase that is comparatively early in the sequences of cultivation noted on the Orme. One series of ridges runs down the slope

Overview of the mining area

towards Pyllau (c). They are overlain by the embankment for the Great
Orme tramway. These are not quite as sharp as the ridges from the system
on the common, suggesting they went out of use somewhat earlier. It may
be significant that these and the ancient ridges at B are also in alignment with
traces of cultivation above Pyllau. Different sectors of the hill went out of
agricultural use at different periods. It is probable that the cessation of
cultivation was because of mining operations.

Agricultural evidence should not be considered in isolation from the mining
activity. When the system of late medieval fields discussed earlier was laid
out on the common, certain areas of Bryniau Poethion were excluded.
Might they have been excluded from the cultivated area because part was
already pitted with trenches and debris from earlier copper-mining activity?
Evidence from agriculture may be pointing to the possibility of some early
copper-mining activity here. There seem to be traces of what may be a faint
line of trials or bellpits running uphill towards the summit (though they
could be natural sinkholes). On one hillock (at D) there are hints of small
circular features resembling those noted at Mynydd Isaf. A faint, small,
square platform (E) might be worth further investigation. A later spoil heap
lies in an earlier rectangular enclosure (F).

Place name evidence may also hold clues. *Bryniau Poethion* means *burnt or scorched hills.* [7] The term *poeth (burnt)* can refer to practices of firing heather (unlikely here) or may be applied to shallow soils that dry out in hot weather (possible) but it might conceivably refer to firesetting practices, or to some early smelting process, or charcoal making. Here if anywhere on the Great Orme, might be the place to start looking for possible evidence of smelting. Certainly the landscape evidence is providing us with a wider context in which to set the mining.

In this book we have examined some of the the aerial evidence for just five complex areas of ancient landscape at Llandudno. There are many other interesting areas. However there is not space to deal with more here. Further aerial photographs are available in the County Archives [7].

There are other small patches of rough ground on the Great Orme which bear traces of cultivation in addition to those investigated in detail here. This area of cultivation lies on rough ground above Pyllau farm.

Just outside of the enclosed area in the south west, is a patch of cultivation ridges. Ancient parallel walls are also visible on the same alignment and may represent some earlier form of land allocation. Under the turf inside the enclosed area faint cuts and scars may indicate former small scale mining or prospecting activity.

11

Agricultural Change on the Great Orme

Early land organisation

THE SUPERB multi-period agricultural landscapes of the Great Orme have not been studied before in the detail they deserve. Aerial photography is particularly suited to the investigation and recording of this sort of evidence. The ancient parallel walls, linear plots, and early cultivation traces do raise questions about the organisation of early agriculture. There is little evidence of square 'Celtic fields', but much for slender linear or rectangular strips. Putting together the fragments of surviving ancient landscape, one wonders if the Great Orme was once divided by broad parallel land divisions, subdivided into narrower linear field systems and plots where intensive arable cultivation took place. (Large scale coaxial land divisions are known in other areas such as Devon and Cornwall.) The evidence for Llandudno is tantalising, because recent agricultural processes have probably erased much earlier evidence. It is on marginal land at the fringes that most evidence survives. But in dry conditions, there are suggestions of narrow strips below the Church, and even within the farmed land of Penmynydd isaf, and other intriguing traces on the main plateau.

The retreat of cultivation and shifting settlement

In view of the role of transhumance in the Welsh uplands, it might have been expected that this isolated plateau would have been a prime area for the seasonal movement of livestock from lowland to upland. But aerial photography reveals the wide extent of former arable on this exposed limestone plateau, even in areas that are highly marginal by today's standards. (The Great Orme is classed as grade 5 agricultural land [1]). In fact a reverse process of transhumance may well have been practised, which is common on other limestone areas such as the Burren in Ireland. Limestone suffers from lack of water in summer, whereas its well drained soils are less prone to damage from livestock in winter. At Llandudno livestock may have been removed to the low lying marshy and sandy areas below the Orme in summer, and returned to the upland, once crops were harvested. Over time some areas went out of cultivation. At Hwylfa'r Ceirw and Mynydd Isaf, and on a part of Bryniau Poethion cultivated areas were abandoned. In more recent times there was further abandonment of a late medieval field system to sheep and cattle pasture.

There has been a shift eastwards. Early settlement is found in the far west near the lighthouse, in what is now an area of extremely denuded soils. Occasional linear boundaries in the far south western areas may even imply that some stony areas there once had more soil cover. The location of the parish church in the north western sector suggests some focus of settlement in the vicinity. It has been demonstrated that at Hwylfa'r Ceirw and perhaps round the church formerly intensively cultivated areas went out of use. In the later medieval period, and in the following centuries the focus of settlement and cultivation shifted further eastwards. The eastern sectors may have had the more fertile soils. Shelter was also probably a factor. There are many different micro-climates on the Great Orme. By the early nineteenth century the main focus of settlement was the mining settlement at Yr Wyddfid, in the eastern sector of the Great Orme. Following the development of the new planned town of Llandudno after 1848, the new town was sited even further eastwards, in an area below the Great Orme itself.

Dating agricultural evidence

All of the agricultural landscapes investigated in the previous chapters represent ancient landscapes. They have long passed out of use, and bear no relation to the present day systems. But is it possible to date them? Dating field systems and traces of cultivation is fraught with pitfalls. Field systems often continued in use for many centuries, spanning perhaps 500 years or even millennia. Association with datable habitation sites or finds of artefacts is the usual method, but this is not always a reliable guide, especially where complex, superimposed agricultural landscapes are found. (Fields may continue to be farmed even when buildings go out of use). Analysis of the field systems and cultivation ridges themselves offers an alternative method. Landscape evidence tells a story of changing patterns of use, even when it is difficult to anchor these sequences firmly in time. In the past any ridge and furrow was vaguely designated as 'medieval', but thanks to the use of aerial photography, it can be appreciated that cultivation can belong to very different periods. Differences between systems of ridges, their alignment, width, organisation and general characteristics, and their degree of weathering can be compared. Some are the result of ploughing. Others result from cultivation by hand.

On the Great Orme there is evidence for a number of phases of agriculture. The occasional survival of superimposed landscapes can provide clues to sequences of agricultural activity. Small narrow linear fields and parallel land divisions may represent an early form of agriculture, perhaps even with prehistoric origins. Other extremely weathered expanses of cultivation may also relate to early agricultural activity. Some cultivation, probably evolving from this, was organized within narrow, linear or rectangular terraced or interlocking arable plots. It is possible to envisage how the interlocking landscape at Hwylfa'r Ceirw might have evolved out of a system of slender parallel land divisions, such as we see at Mynydd Isaf, modified by periodic reallocation and on-going intensive activity over a long period in a core agricultural area under permanent cultivation. Such areas might have been farmed by a bond community. Recent work of early medieval historians such as Professor G. R. J. Jones suggests that post-Roman society consisted of a largely bond population with a crust of notables and nobles [2]. Vestiges of narrow strips also existed at Gogarth and Yr Wyddfid, both bond townships. The system on the common probably represents a later medieval system, and is on a different axis to some earlier cultivation.

Why did things change?

Field patterns tend to persist for many centuries. Agricultural change may occur because of technological change. The introduction of new methods of ploughing, for instance may have led to a lengthening of strips. Changed field patterns might be a result of a desertion followed by recolonization, or may result after a temporary reversion of the land to pastoral use. Occasionally change may come from a deliberate reorganisation by a powerful landowner. Change can also occur when existing systems come under stress or break down. Different systems might even conceivably co-exist for a period in adjacent areas. A free and a bond system might be differently organized, and produce different landscape forms.

Which of these might account for the change on the Great Orme? One could produce any number of plausible explanations. Desertion or withdrawal of populations and livestock could have occurred during the struggle with the invading Normans. This was an area that was one of the most hotly contested in the prolonged struggle over more than 200 years between the Normans and Welsh, and nearby Deganwy castle changed hands several times. The later Welsh Princes could have reorganized land tenure. After 1150 they are known to have modernized their state and remodelled and reorganized many holdings. Or new agricultural practices (perhaps modelled on the English manorial system) might have taken root following the Edwardian conquest of north Wales, perhaps after the grant of Gogarth to the Bishop of Bangor, known for his love of Anglicized ways and lifestyles. The effects of the Black Death or the wars of Glyndŵr might also have led to change, although this would seem to be rather too late in the timescale.

Let us look more closely at the first detailed documentary evidence offered by the *Record of Caernarvon,* the Welsh 'Domesday' survey [3]. There are clues here which may imply that a major reorganisation of land could have taken place before the Edwardian conquest of Gwynedd. To understand the wider context we need to look elsewhere in the Creuddyn peninsular in the very early thirteenth century. Several writers have drawn attention to the problems faced by the last Welsh princes in getting fighting men who could go to war for long periods outside the boundaries of Gwynedd (something the traditional feudal obligations did not cover). To overcome this problem the Princes seem to have created new forms of tenure and a new privileged class of freemen. In return for substantial privileges such as rent free tenancies, certain freemen were contracted to go to war with the lord prince. Land reorganisation is known to have occurred in Anglesey where it was especially associated with descendants of Llywelyn's seneschal, Ednyfed Fychan [4]. There is evidence for a substantial reorganisation in Creuddyn also, ascribed to Llywelyn Fawr in the very early thirteenth century. In Creuddyn at Gloddaeth, Penrhyn and Trefwarth new townships of freemen, contracted to go to war with the Prince, were created. Such an arrangement was also extremely useful for defensive purposes. The Creuddyn peninsula was a strategic area, controlling the crossing of the lower Conwy and access into the heartland of Gwynedd along the coastal lowland route. One effect of the prince's reorganisation was to place what has been described as 'a protective shield of freemen' around the borders of Creuddyn [5].

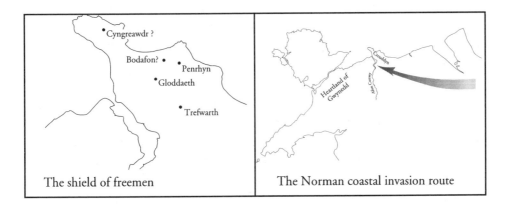

| The shield of freemen | The Norman coastal invasion route |

The township of Cyngreawdr

Although the Survey makes no mention of any military service in respect of the township of Cyngreawdr, many of the other characteristics of these distinctive new free townships are there. The inhabitants enjoy a highly privileged status: the status of freemen, freedom from paying rent, ('They owe nothing except suit of court' states the survey), lack of burdensome dues and services, and a degree of jurisdictional freedom. The free tenants of Cyngreawdr also had their own under-tenants, who might even have been people of bond status. The existence of considerable numbers of bond under-tenants may lie concealed in the post conquest surveys. Significantly freemen at nearby Bodafon township also had under-tenants, [6]. It is true that not all freemen rode to war with the Prince, but the creation of some free tenancies may have had the effect of placing crucial areas in dependable hands. many of the reforms of the later Welsh Princes, social, economic and military, had the same strategic objective of strengthening the kingdom to secure its survival. After 1150 there is evidence that considerable numbers of free tenancies were being granted in many areas of Gwynedd. The fields on the common may represent the lands farmed ny free tenants of Cyngreawdr, although it is, of course, extremely difficult to correlate medieval surveys with exact geographic locations.

Later change

How might we account for the subsequent abandonment of the western most part of this strip system? The strips of the township must have been in use for some considerable period to explain the build-up of such prominent ridges on the common. They were almost certainly cultivated for hundreds of years. It is unlikely, therefore, that their abandonment in this case was due to the Black Death, the pestilence which struck north Wales in 1352, or to the effects of the Glyndŵr rebellion, 1400 to circa 1410. (This is not to say the area was unaffected by such events.) Contraction of arable farming on the summit plateau might have been influenced by climatic changes. After 1300, the climate became progressively colder, culminating (with some fluctuations) in an extremely cold period in the seventeenth century [7].

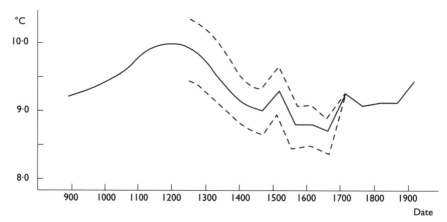

Changing patterns of climate (after H. L. Lamb); dotted lines show range of uncertainty.

Deterioration of climate occurred at the same time as other trends were
encouraging a move towards cattle and sheep raising. There were both push
and pull factors. New markets for Welsh wool and cattle developed under
the Tudors and Stuarts. Welsh drovers were expanding the cattle trade with
London, bringing in valuable income to the Welsh economy. The fine, well
drained pastureland on the Great Orme would have been particularly
attractive for stock rearing. At Llandudno in the later sixteenth century
freeholders and tenants seem to have profiteered by allowing outsiders, who
did not hold land in the parish, to pasture sheep and cattle on the Orme. [8]
This seems to have led to severe overgrazing of the wastes, so much so that
after 1598 grazing practices had to be strictly regulated. Only tenants and
freeholders with lands in the manor were allowed to pasture livestock on the
wastes and commons, and then in accordance with strict quotas

> 'after the rate and according to the quantitie of suche landes as he hathe of
> his owne freehold or such landes as is to him leased'.

With such lucrative new markets and strong pressures towards stock-raising,
coupled with a deteriorating climate affecting crop-growing, it is possible to
envisage a decision to allow some of the poorer land to revert to pasture.
Possibly therefore the lands on the common went out of cultivation towards
the end of the sixteenth century. But human decisions can be just as
important as environmental factors. Not all the land was abandoned to
common pasture. The Mostyns, emerging as a new and powerful family,
seem to have pursued an independent policy in the lands they had acquired.
Indeed field name evidence for the Mostyn-owned Penmynydd farm suggests
that a mixed farming policy was adopted there, with certain fields being
allocated for meadow (*Dôl Isa, Dôl Ucha, the lower and upper meadows)*, and
other land designated as arable *(Cae Ceirch, the oatfield)* [9].

Eventually estate building by the Mostyn family led to the creation of
'closes', and to the process of enclosing and blocking up parcels of land to
form more compact units. In Gogarth township as early as 1482 a 'close',
Cae Meirch, is mentioned in a deed [10], although this was probably an
enclosure carved out of the wastes on the marshy land below the Orme.
Enclosing of the open fields came rather later. In 1614 the holding of Maes y
Facrell was still being delineated in a deed of mortgage by its relationship to

other holdings [11], suggesting that it was still unenclosed. The enclosure process may have taken place later in the seventeenth century, for certainly by 1680, the process was well advanced. Better control over valuable mineral rights may also have been an important motive.

Much later, the 1847 Parliamentary Enclosure completed the process on the Great Orme, instigated by powerful landowners who wanted free reign to improve and develop their lands. A crucial factor then may have been the Mostyn family's desire to develop a new resort at Llandudno, for it is remarkable how much land in key sectors came into Mostyn control as a result of the Enclosure, and how quickly the development of a fashionable seaside resort at Llandudno began.

Landscape change at Llandudno

To summarise, a number of key points emerge from the areas we have investigated:

- There has been a shrinkage of the area under cultivation.
- There has been a drift of farming and settlement eastwards.
- From the surviving landscape evidence it is possible to distinguish several phases of agricultural activity on the Great Orme.
- In places cultivation has been superseded by mining.

It has also been possible to propose approximate dates for certain of the later major landscape changes that have occurred at Llandudno, based on inferences from the scanty documentary evidence that survives:

- Some reorganisation of tenure took place at Cyngreawdr, probably in the later twelfth or thirteenth century and land there was given to freemen.
- Some of the freemen's lands were abandoned to common pasture, possibly towards the end of the sixteenth century because of the growing importance of cattle and sheep raising, and as a result of the activities of the Welsh drovers, coupled with a deterioration in the climate.
- Modern, compact, enclosed farms appeared on the Great Orme in the seventeenth century.

12

The Landscape of Mining

The contribution of aerial photography

O<small>N THE GROUND</small> industrial areas can be confusing to all but the industrial archaeologist. Only experts after careful survey may be able to make sense of the remains. Aerial photographs of mining landscapes allow the remains of industry to be appreciated by a far wider audience. One aerial photograph can be worth many pages of description. From the air we can see the patterns made by, for example, lines of bell pits, and can more easily appreciate the way they follow a seam or outcrop. Aerial photographs provide a valuable record of industrial sites. The overview provided by aerial photography gives a time-depth to industrial activity. We can sometimes appreciate sequences of activity or contrasting mining techniques. We also see the industrial site in a wider context, and can better appreciate the impact of industrial activity on the surrounding landscape.

Industrial sites are at particularly risk to later clearance. Aerial photography can provide a permanent record even after site clearance has taken place. It is important to preserve any available photography in a permanent archive. Valuable as written documents are they tell only part of the story. Maps and plans are useful, but they give only a 'snapshot' at a particular point in time, and frequently leave out redundant features or data not relevant to their own purposes. Nineteenth century maps of Pyllau focused on contemporary features, the buildings and deep mining shafts, yet as the aerial photographs have demonstrated, there is a wealth of evidence for a great deal of other, probably earlier activity, not recorded on the maps.

Small scale activity and surface exploitation

The history of intensive, heavily capitalized deep mining of the eighteenth and nineteenth centuries at Llandudno has been well covered by several excellent studies. Chris Williams has extensively covered the available documentary evidence[1]. Duncan James in the 1970s and Don Smith and other members of the Great Orme Exploration Society and A. Lewis in the later 1980s and 90s have explored and written about the fascinating subterranean evidence of mining at Llandudno and have carefully mapped the deep mines[2]. More recently Bronze Age mining activity has been the subject of intensive archaeological investigation by Gwynedd Archaeological Trust and the Great Orme Mines Ltd. [3]. Smaller scale mining activity has not yet received as much attention, though there is, as has been shown, surviving field evidence in several places on the Great Orme. Aerial photography may be a method particularly suited to recording this type of trace evidence. Only an aerial photograph can do justice to the complexity of the activity on Bryniau Poethion, or the multi-period evidence at Pyllau.

This book has deliberately focused on five areas which offer useful case studies. It is not feasible here to publish photographs of every location with traces of mining activity. The wider photographic record has been deposited in the county archives. Some of the traces are very slight indeed. Sometimes ground disturbance shows up better on infra red film than on conventional photography. Dry weather has also revealed suggestions of mining activity and areas of debris or ground disturbance, for instance on the main plateau above Gogarth. There are many small, shallow cuttings just a few metres wide. Some evidence may represent the work of only a few seasons. Much is probably exploitation of surface outcrops. This sort of low key activity forms part of the story of mining at Llandudno and has left an imprint on the landscape. To the social and landscape historian interested in human subsistence in a marginal area, it is part of the story of how Llandudno's former inhabitants wrested a living on an unpromising limestone headland. Indeed in the landscapes of the Great Orme we have a spectrum of mining techniques, from the primitive to the highly sophisticated. This is what makes it such a remarkable area. Bell pits and small scale trenches, cuttings and dumps are very different in character from the heavily capitalized

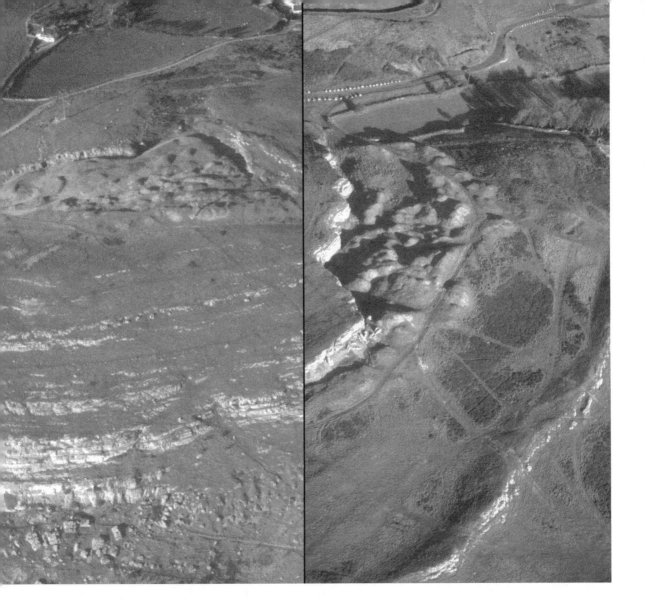

This book has tended to focus on copper-mining, which was the major industry at Llandudno. Stone quarries were of course another important form of industrial activity here. Limestone was prized for building. It is known that limestone from the quarry above Craig Rofft (left) was used in the construction of Conwy bridge [4], and the other quarry above Pyllau (right) was noted for its fossils. The two galleries illustrated here may even have seen some open cast extraction as well as stone quarrying, or their tips may have been reworked for traces of ore [5]. Some of the dumps are more reminiscent of mining landscapes than of conventional fan shaped quarry tips. There was also a sandpit, beside the quarried area in the left hand photograph. A small square structure is faintly visible in the older part of the working. In the farmland behind, under bushes, is spoil from a trial or mine.

nineteenth century mine sites, but taken together they offer valuable information about ways in which mining in Wales developed. Some sites may also preserve evidence of earlier mining.

Both the evidence for small scale activity, and the indications that some highly productive areas and tips have been worked and reworked, does raise questions about the current view of a complete cessation of mining at Llandudno between the end of the Bronze Age or Roman occupation and the industrial period. Lewis noted possible traces of pick cut gouges in underground caverns under Pyllau, suggesting a re-working with iron tools at a later date [5]. Roman mining activity at Llandudno has in the past been inferred from extremely circumstantial evidence, (based chiefly on Roman finds in the vicinity of Llandudno, rather than on the Great Orme plateau). What then is one to make of the abundant, widespread evidence on the Great Orme for agriculture and settlement in the Dark Age and later medieval period? Was there such a complete cessation of mining activity, between the third or fourth centuries and the late seventeenth century, as has generally been alleged? Might there have been intermittent, small scale activity perhaps exploiting outcrops, shallow workings, or reworking older sites? Although there is little sign of a money economy in the early Christian period, the arrival of the Vikings and Normans introduced significant economic change. Viking activity turned the Irish Sea basin into a trading area. Our knowledge of their activities has been enhanced by excavations in Dublin in the 1980s. Indeed among the coppersmiths of Viking Dublin there would have been a ready market for small quantities of copper. After 1283, too, it is possible to envisage some role for small scale mining or surface working or to provide cash in a new money economy. Mining could have been an occasional, part-time, seasonal activity to supplement farming. Further investigation is needed.

Mining and agriculture should not be compartmentalized. Frequently they illuminate each other. Perhaps one of the greatest contributions of aerial photography is to demonstrate how agricultural and mining landscapes at Llandudno interlock and overlie each other. One can see how, at location after location, industry superseded cultivation.

13

Postscript

Summary

THE FRESH viewpoint afforded by aerial photography provides valuable evidence and illustration of human activity on the Great Orme during several millennia. This book has examined five chosen areas of historic landscape on the Great Orme using aerial photography. Remarkable expanses of former ancient landscape are still preserved. These can be plotted. They yield valuable evidence about agricultural practice, desertion and changing land use. Some landscape evidence may relate to early activity from a prehistoric or Roman period. There is abundant landscape evidence of agriculture during the early and later medieval period. A former bond community may have been followed by free tenants of the township of Cyngreawdr. In the more recent period there has been a marked shift of settlement and activity eastward, with western areas being largely abandoned. In several of the areas studied, historic agricultural landscapes are overlain with debris from later mining activity. The book provides an overview of selected areas of mining activity. As well as mining activity in the Bronze Age and highly capitalized mining of the industrial period, there is evidence for scattered smaller scale activity

Evidence from the landscape

There is an unwritten history etched into the Welsh landscape, and aerial photography can help us to read and interpret that story. Llandudno's limestone headland seen from the air contains some remarkable historic

areas. Here is a spectrum of mining techniques, perhaps unique in Britain.
This is set within a far wider landscape context providing visible evidence of
multi-period agricultural and settlement activity. At the time of writing,
interesting developments are taking place which are rapidly extending our
knowledge of early mining history. There is however, a real need for
examination of the broader context of agriculture, land use and other human
activity against which to place the industrial activity on the Great Orme.

A key purpose of the book has been to draw attention to the wealth of
surviving historic landscape at Llandudno. Aerial photography is a powerful
medium for landscape history research. More important even than its ability
to provide superb illustrations is its ability to demonstrate the relationship of
different features to each other and to provide a time depth to the landscape
which helps us to understand processes of landscape change.

The way forward

The historic landscape on the Great Orme is heritage under threat. In the
past it was on-going agricultural usage, particularly deep ploughing activity,
that caused the greatest loss of archaeological evidence. Now the situation is
different. Large areas of the remaining open land on the Great Orme have
recently been given over to tourists as a great leisure park. Perhaps the threat
to Llandudno's historic landscapes comes now from the pressures of tourism
and visitor numbers. Former industrial landscapes can be particularly at risk.
They are often threatened by 'landscaping' activity or the development of
amenity spaces such as car parks and picnic areas for which huge derelict
land grants are available. The word 'eyesore' is often used, and their historic
value can go unrecognized. To an extent this has already happened at
Llandudno. Field systems and cultivation traces are also far more at risk than
more conventional archaeological 'sites and monuments'. Pressures from
cars parking on the grass of the open common, over the remains of historic
field systems above the church, for instance, must surely cause loss and
damage over time. The sheer pressure of tourism and visitor numbers
treating the area as an outdoor activity area may in the long term result in
erosion and damage. Llandudno will need to address the problems of
conserving and managing its areas of surviving historic landscape. Perhaps

the first step is to recognize their existence and their unique significance. A remarkable multi-period landscape survives on the Great Orme. Locked up in the landscape evidence of field banks, traces of cultivation, pits and spoil heaps is the story of human activity on the Great Orme over several millennia. This is a valuable part of the heritage of the local community, and it is also a part of the wider heritage of Wales. We hold this in trust and it ought to be preserved.

Tourist paths cause significant erosion on Mynydd Isaf. Compare this photograph taken in 1995 with the one page 78 taken a decade earlier

Acknowledgements

FIRSTLY I owe a special debt of gratitude to my husband, Capell, who has been my pilot or co-pilot on the many sorties we have done together. He has also been responsible for the design of this book which was wholly generated on computer. The computer-generated plots, maps and diagrams are also gratefully acknowledged as his work.

We have also received considerable technical assistance and advice from Pro-vision of Leeds and T. J. Reproductions of West Hampstead, London. I must also thank my flying instructors, and most particularly Bill Shepherd and Roy Hodder, for their patience and effort in teaching me to fly, and all the many members of Mona Flying Club who have given encouragement to my research and flying over the years. Mr Bryn Parry of the Gwynedd Archives and Museums Service kindly allowed me time to attend meetings of the Aerial Archaeology Research Group and the Council for British Archaeology's Aerial Archaeology Committee for which I am most grateful. I am grateful also to many members of these two organisations for sharing their expertise and advice, and for commenting on some photographs. Special thanks are due to Chris Musson of the National Monuments Record, Aberystwyth, for his help and encouragement. Many other specialists have offered advice or have been prepared to discuss specific issues with me, including Stephen Briggs of the Royal Commission, Aberystwyth, members of Gwynedd Archaeological Trust and Great Orme Mines, and Adam Sharpe and other members of the Cornwall Archaeology unit. Thanks are also due to Tomos Roberts of the University Manuscripts Department, Bangor, for his advice on placenames. Several other people have looked at the manu-script and given helpful advice. All mistakes and other deficiencies however are entirely my own.

In researching this book I have drawn on material gleaned from documents and reference material in the County Archives. Items on pages 25, 28, 34, 40, and 42 are from the collections of Gwynedd Archives Service.

The flying and reconnaissance programme has been carried out entirely without public funding or financial support of any kind, as part of a personal research project, over a number of years, to investigate and record the historic landscapes of Gwynedd.

Notes and References

Chapter 1

1] W. G. Hoskins, *Fieldwork and Local History*, Faber, 1968.

Chapter 2

1] Much of this chapter is based on information from Ivor E. Davies, 'The Geology of the Creuddyn Peninsular', *Journal of Llandudno Historical Society and Field Club*, 1923.
2] Report on the Old Mine 1848, N.L.W. Bangor Diocesan records, B/EP/185.
3] H. T. Williams, *Newsletter of the Llandudno Historical Society*, no. 1, 1989.
4] Series of interviews with ex copper-miner John Hughes, *Llandudno Advertiser*, 30 June, 7 July, and 14 July 1917.
5] A. Lewis, (in 'Underground Exploration of the Great Orme Copper-Mines', *Early Mining in Wales*, editors P. Crew and S. Crew, Plas Tan y Bwlch Occasional Papers no. 1, Porthmadog 1990) remarks on the similarity of some caverns to natural cave passages, but tends to discount this. Stephen Briggs of the National Monuments Commission, Aberystwyth, has suggested that *some* caverns may be of natural origin enlarged by mining activity (C. S. Briggs, 'Prehistoric Mining Mania', 1994, forthcoming).

Chapter 3

1] D. Fraser suggests in *Land and Society in Neolithic Orkney*, British Archaeological Reports, 1985 that neolithic burial chambers were far more than houses for the dead and had a function as territorial markers: *'The right of a group of people to use a particular area of land was legitimized by the presence thereon of the remains of the ancestors of that people. A group of people regarded themselves as belonging to a particular patch of land. In order to mark the relationship permanently they constructed a monument on that land.'* Burial monuments were often placed on the edge of a cultivated area. Possibly therefore the area of earliest farming and settlement on the Great Orme itself may have been somewhere near Yr Wyddfid.
2] H. Ellis, *The Record of Caernarvon*, London, 1838.
3] Douglas B. Hague, 'The Bishop's Palace at Gogarth', *Transactions of Caernarvonshire Historical Society*, 1956.
4] *Record of Caernarvon*, op. cit. Originally the survey was dated to the 1348/9, but D. Stephenson in *The Governance of Gwynedd*, p. 93, has now used internal evidence to date the Gogarth sections of the survey to 1306. I am also most grateful to Tomos Roberts of the University Manuscripts Department, Bangor, for his guidance concerning the many versions of the township name Cyngreawdr. This appears in many forms but the spelling favoured by the late Professor Melville Richards has been used throughout this book.
5] T. Jones Pierce, 'Some tendencies in the Agrarian History of Caernarvonshire', *Transactions of*

Caernarvonshire Historical Society, 1939, and W. H. Walters, 'The Making of Caernarvonshire', *Transactions of Caernarvonshire Historical Society*, 1942/3.

6] Douglas B. Hague, op. cit.

7] T. Jones Pierce, op. cit.

8] N.L.W. Thorne MSS 250

9] N.L.W. Thorne MSS 112, 141–3, 146, 203.

10] N.L.W. Thorne MSS 11, 17, 72, 209, 287.

11] N.L.W. Bangor Diocesan records, B/EP/447

12] UCNW Mostyn MSS 7033

13] Peter Bailey Williams, *Caernarvonshire,* Caernarvon, 1820. and Thomas Pennant *Tours in Wales,* 1777

14] C. J. Williams, *The Llandudno Copper-Mines,* Northern Mines Research Society, 1979, p. 10, and *Llandudno Historical Society Newsletter,* No. 1, p. 18, 1989.

Chapter 4

1] Much of the archaeological information in this chapter and chapters 5 and 6 is drawn from information held by Gwynedd Archaeological Trust and from discussions with staff on site at the Great Orme Mines Ltd. Full acknowledgment is also made of information in: Danny Dutton, 'Early Mining on the Great Orme', *From Magic to Merchandise—the Search for Metals*; notes and lecture at Clwyd Archaeological Day School 1993; and of *Early Mining in the British Isles,* editors P. Crew and S. Crew, op. cit.

2] C. S. Briggs, 'Some Processes and Problems in Later Prehistoric Wales and Beyond', *L'Age du Bronze Atlantique,* editors Christian Cheviollet and André Coffyn, Association des Musées du Salardais, 1991.

3] *'The Great Orme mining complex seems to be on a scale unprecedented in this age of any mineral exploitation in western Europe',* A. Lewis, 'Underground Exploration of the Great Orme', P. Crew and S. Crew, op. cit. See also A. Hammond, 'The Great Orme Mine', *Current Archaeology,* vol. 130, 1992, 404–9.

4] P. Budd, D. Gale, A. M. Pollard, R. G. Thomas, P. A. Williams, 'Early Mines in Wales—a Reconsideration', *Archaeology in Wales,* 1992.

5] O. Davies, 'The Copper-Mines on the Great Orme's Head', *Archaeologia Cambrensis,* 1938.

6] Harri Gwynn Jones, 'The Llandudno Copper-Mines in the Eighteenth Century', *Bulletin of the Board of Celtic Studies,* 1939, and UCNW Porth yr Aur MSS 30657–60.

7] *Llandudno Advertiser,* 1917, op.cit.

Chapter 5

1] *Llandudno Advertiser,* 1917, op. cit.

2] ibid.

3] N.L.W. Bangor Diocesan Records, B/EP/185

4] Danny Dutton, and Gwynedd Archaeological Trust, op. cit.

5] C. J. Williams, op. cit.

6] *Llandudno Advertiser,* 1917, op. cit.

7] G.A.M.S. X/AMP/4

8] *Llandudno Advertiser,* 1917, op.cit.

9] 'The Great Orme', *Journal of Llandudno Historical Society and Field Club,* 1909/10.

10] *Llandudno Advertiser*, 1917, op.cit.

11] Willoughby Gardiner, 'Some finds of Roman coins in Creuddyn', in W. B. Lowe, *Heart of Northern Wales*, 1912

12] J. Bryan Hope, *A Curious Place—The Industrial History of Amlwch*, 1994.

13] T. Craddock, 'Copper Smelting in Bronze Age Britain, problems and possibilities' in P. Crew and S. Crew, op cit.

14] Arthur Aiken, *A Tour of North Wales*, 1797.

Chapter 6

1] C. J. Williams, op. cit.

2] O. Davies, op. cit.

3] UCNW Mostyn papers 7028.

4] ex info Danny Dutton of Gwynedd Archaeological Trust and staff of Great Orme Mines Ltd.

5] see the series of notes and articles on early mining and the Great Orme in *Archaeology in Wales* by C. S. Briggs, 1988, 1991; A. Lewis, 1989; L. Dutton, 1991; C. G. Davies, 1992, P. Budd and others, 1992.

6] Some archaeologists have postulated Bronze Age mining activity on a massive scale at Llandudno, taking out large quantities of highest quality ores—A. Lewis 'Underground Exploration of the Great Orme Copper-Mines', P. Crew and S. Crew, op.cit. It has also been suggested that the mines here were virtually worked out by the end of the Bronze Age, until a new process of smelting encouraged the working of the sulphide ores, Duncan James, 'Prehistoric copper-mines on the Great Orme's Head', P. Crew and S. Crew op.cit.

7] *Llandudno Advertiser*, 1917 op.cit.

8] Danny Dutton, G.A.T. op.cit.

Chapter 7

1] Map in Williams, *Llandudno its History and Natural History*, Llandudno, 1861.

2] Map of mines and caves at Llandudno prepared by C. A. Lewis, 1988, kindly supplied by the Great Orme Exploration Society.

3] *Journal of Llandudno Historical Society and Field Club*, 1909–10, op.cit.

4] Article in *Caernarvon and Denbigh Herald*, 23 May 1849.

5] I am grateful to Mrs C. J. Cornwell, Town Clerk of Llandudno, and to other members of the Town Council for this information.

Chapter 8

1] A useful account of the formation of ridge and furrow is offered in Michael Aston, *Interpreting the Landscape*, Batsford, 1985.

2] ex info Frances Lynch, Department of Archaeology, UCNW Bangor.

3] *Caernarvon and Denbigh Herald*, 1849, op.cit.

4] 'St Tudno's Church', *Archaeologia Cambrensis*, 1912, p. 147.

5] G.A.M.S. XQA / Llandudno Enclosure Award.

6] Edmund Hyde Hall, *A Description of Caernarvonshire*, 1809, p. 55, Caernarvonshire Historical Society, 1968.

7] I am grateful to Andrew Davison of Gwynedd Archaeological Trust for discussing the matter.

Chapter 9

1] Note by C. A. Lewis, *Archaeology in Wales*, 1990.

2] ibid.

3] *Journal of Llandudno Historical Society and Field Club*, 1909–10, op.cit.

4] H. Savoury, 'The Late Bronze Age in Wales, new Discoveries and Interpretation', *Archaeologia Cambrensis*, 1958, p. 14–15.

Chapter 10

1] C. J. Wiliams, op.cit.

2] *Caernarvon and Denbigh Herald*, 1849 op.cit.

3] G.A.M.S. XM/ 1758.

4] Don Williams, *The Great Orme Copper-Mines*, Creuddyn Publications, 1988.

5] Harri Gwynn Jones, op.cit.

6] Royal Commission on Ancient and Historical Monuments, *Caernarvonshire—East*, HMSO, 1953.

7] G.A.M.S. XD/ 80

8] Tomos Roberts of the UCNW Manuscripts Department kindly offered advice on placenames.

Chapter 11

1] *Atlas of Caernarvonshire*, ed. T. M. Basset, Gwyrfai Rural Council, 1973.

2] G. R. J. Jones, 'The Distribution of Bond Settlement in North West Wales', *Welsh History Review*, 1964.

3] *Record of Caernarvon*, op.cit.

4] Glyn Roberts, 'Wyrion Eden—the Anglesey descendents of Ednyfed Fychan in the fourteenth century', *Aspects of Welsh History*, University of Wales Press, 1969.

5] Anthony Carr, 'Medieval Gloddaeth', *Transactions of Caernarvonshire Historical Society*, 1977; also unpublished MA thesis by G. R. J. Jones, 'The military Geography of Creuddyn in the thirteenth century', University of Wales, 1949.

6] G. R. J. Jones, 1964, op cit.

7] A detailed discussion of climate changes can be found in H. H. Lamb, *Climate, History and the Modern World*, Methuen, 1982.

8] N.L.W. Thorne MSS 218, 179, 180.

9] G.A.M.S. Tithe schedule, Llandudno, 1840. Presumably many fields were named in the seventeenth century (see Thorne MSS), before eighteenth century ideas on crop rotation became prevalent,

10] N.L.W. Thorne MSS 147

11] N.L.W. Thorne MSS 225

Chapter 12

1] C. J. Williams, op.cit.

2] Duncan James, op.cit.; Don Williams, op.cit.

3] Danny Dutton and Tony Lewis, op. cit.

4] Ivor Wynne Jones, Llandudno, *Queen of the Welsh Resorts*, Cardiff, 1975. See also H. Provis, *The*

Britannia and Conway Bridges, London, 1850.

5] O. Davies in 1939 noted *'nearly on the top of the hill . . . a roughly cut gallery, of uncertain date, following a line of brecciated limestone, which presumably accompanied a thin vein'*. This may even be the work noted by Aiken near the summit, where a seam a few inches thick was being worked.

Legend to diagrams

 cultivation ridges

 cultivation ridges barely discernible

 lines of old walls

 traces of old walls

 rough ground from mining activity

 pits, bell pits

 other mining activity

 scarp

 roads or trackways

 wells

Index

Illustrations and photographs are indicated by bold type

Aiken, A. 43, 48

Bingley, W. 33, 60, 72
Bishop of Bangor 21, 23, 25, 33, 92
    Anian 21
Black Death 23, 92, 94
Bryn Euryn 20, 45–47
Bryniau Poethion 36, 38, 55, **82**–87, 90

cattle farming 90, 95, 96
caverns 16, **18**, 30, 56, 85, 100
climate 90, 94–96
closes 25, 95
common land 8, **67**–73, 83, 86, 91, 94–95,
    102
Craig Rofft 99
cultivation ridges 57, 61, 71, 85, 88, 91
    mapped 54, 58, 63, 69, 73, 76, 83
    photographs **9, 54, 58, 62, 64, 68, 73,
    74, 76, 82, 87, 88**
    see also ploughing, spade cultivation
Cyngreawdr 21, 22, 24, 93–94, 96, 101

Domesday Book 21
drovers 95, 96

earthworks 73, 75
    see also hillforts
Edward I 21–22
enclosures 25–26, **28**, 33, 42, 53, 57, 59, 61,
    63, 64, 66, 71, 74, 78, 86, 95, 96

field systems 8, **24**, 26, **58**, 61, 63, 67–70,
    78, 85, 90, 91, 102
freemen 92–94, 96

Garthgogo, Abergele 20
Gloddaeth 24–**25**, 36, 93
Glyndŵr, Owain 20, 23, 49, 92, 94
Gogarth 15, 20–26, 31, 40, 51, 91–92, 95
Gruffudd ap Rhys 24

Hague, Douglas 20
hillforts **19, 20, 45**
    see also earthworks
Hwylfa'r Ceirw 8, **58**, 59–66, 69, 73, 75,
    78, 90, 91
Hyde Hall, E. 74

Industrial Revolution 32, 51, 53
Iron Age 19

John Hughes, miner 16, 33, 36, 44, 46, 55,
    56
John Jones, Maes y Garnedd 24

Kendrick's cave 19

Llety Fadog 60, 63–64
Llety'r Filiast 19
Llywelyn Fawr 93–94, 96
Llwyn Helyg 25
Llys Helig 20

Maes y Facrell 19, 25, 26, 55, 95
Margaret ferch Gruffudd 24
mining:
  bell pits 38, **68**, **76**, 77, 78, **79**, 80,
    82–86, **87**, 97, 98
  brammock rods 40, **41**, **42**
  Bronze Age mines **50**, 51, 57
  deep mines 33, 53, 98
  engines 33, 37, 39–41, 53, 55–56
  levels 32–33, 37, 39, 56, 74, 80, 85
  mining village **27**
  prospecting **35**, 56, 74, 78, 83, 98
  shafts 37–40, 53, 55–56, 84–85, 97
  slime pits 44, **54**, 56
  small scale mining 14, 59, 64–65, 77, 88,
    98, 100
  spoil heaps 29, 51, 56, 64, 74, 78, 80, 86,
    99, 103
  Vivian shaft 37, 55
  see also caverns, ore processing, quarries,
    smelting
  whimseys **39**, **40**
Morris, W. 26, 32
Mostyn Family 24–26, 28, 33, 95–96
Mynydd Isaf **76**–81, 86, 90, 91

Normans 20, 92, 93, 94, 100

ore processing **43**, 56, 65–66, 77, 78, 81

Parc 28, 64
Pen y Corddin 20
Penmorfa 33, 80
Penmynydd 25, 70, 95
Penmynydd Isaf 70
Penmynydd Uchaf 71, 99
Pennant, T. 26, 63, 60
ploughing 10, 24, 26, 36, 55, 65, 67, 78,
    91, 92, 102
Porth Helyg **79**–80
Pyllau 15, 18, 25, 26, 33, 37, 41, **50**–57, 59,
    74, 80, 86, 88, 97, 98, 100

quarries 10, 77, **99**

Record of Caernarvon 21, 92
Romans 19, 30, 31, 45–48, 81, 84, 91, 100,
    101

Saint Tudno's Church 15, 21, 67–75
settlements **19**, **21**, 26, 29, 31, 67, 70,
    77–79, 90
sheep farming 26, 67, 71, 90, 95–96
smelting 32, 37, 44–48, 80, 87
spade cultivation 61, 69

transhumance 89–90
transport 40, 42, 44–46, 81
  roads 55
  trackways **45**, 53, 75, 81
  see also drovers
Tŷ Gwyn 33
Ty'n-y-coed 25
Ty'n yr Hendre 25

Vikings 100

wars 20–21, 23, 24, 32, 49, 92–93
wells 17, **43**–44, 65–66, 81
  Ffynnon Galchog 44, 81
  Ffynnon Rufeinig 44, **64**, 65
Welsh California 84
Welsh Princes 20, 22, 92
windmills 21, 22, 39
Yr Wyddfid 21–22, 26–**27**, 90, 91